The Sound of Many Waters

By Peter Powell

The Fieldgate Press

The Sound of Many Waters

Peter Powell was born in Dublin in 1939 and educated at Blackrock College.

He started his career in 1958 with the Provincial Bank of Ireland Ltd., with whom he worked for eight years before going on to University College Dublin to read geology.

His career as a mining geologist took him to South Africa (gold), the North Yorkshire Moors of England (potash), and twice to mines in Ireland (zinc/lead). His final position was chief mine geologist at Tara Mines Ltd. near Navan, Co. Meath. He has recently retired.

From very early times Peter's passion was fishing. Sea fishing in Dunmore East, pike fishing in the midland lakes, and trout fishing all over the country absorbed most of his leisure time.

He has been vice chairman of the Ormonde Anglers in Nenagh, Co. Tipperary, and a member of many other angling groups.

This is an account of his huge enthusiasm for fishing and all things related.

Peter played rugby with Blackrock College RFC and is also a keen golfer and current member of Headfort Golf Club in Kells, Co. Meath.

He and his wife Gillian live in Athboy, Co. Meath and they have four grown-up children, two Lakeland terriers and two black cats.

A Fieldgate Paperback
First published in Ireland by The Fieldgate Press 2000
Reprinted 2001

The Fieldgate Press
Kells, Co. Meath.
Tel: +353-46-32571, +353-46-54211 Fax: +353-46-54211
© Peter Powell, 2000

Extract from The Song of the May Fairy taken from FLOWER
FAIRIES OF THE SPRING by Cicely Mary Barker.
Copyright © The Estate of Cicely Mary Barker, 1923.
Reproduced by kind permission of Frederick Warne & Co.

ISBN
0 9534790 3 X

Reprint sponsored by Glen Dimplex

Printed by Offex, John Street, Kells, Co. Meath.

For Clare

Acknowledgements

It has been a pleasure to write this book and in so doing to enjoy again the company of many fishing friends from down the years. They were great times and I wouldn't have missed them for the world.

I thank especially, Michael Crowe, Ruaidhrí de Barra, Val Demery, David Greaves, Al Herriott, George Herriott, Michael Herriott, Charlie Hynes, John Joyce, Davy McBride, Margaret McGrath, Pat McGrath, Peter Milne, Sean Monaghan, Teddy Morgan, Jim O'Ryan, Dick Powell, Pat Sanders, Bernard Sanders and Joe Shea.

My children, Stephanie, David, Nicola and Elva, and my wife Gillian, were a great encouragement to me and kept me writing when the doubts set in. Their honest and constructive criticism substantially shaped the book and I am very grateful to them.

I also thank Pat Rathborne and David Bowes for their advice and much-appreciated support.

I am indebted to my publisher Jim McAleese for his guidance and advice, and to my printer Ben Smyth for his enduring patience.

I owe a great deal to my late stepfather Claude Allman for the exciting fishing holidays in Dunmore East, and for steering many a family outing towards river or lake.

And to my late mother Clare, the catalyst without whom none of this might have happened, I am forever grateful.

Contents

Illustrations

Colour Section

Prologue

It was nine o'clock on a soft, warm evening in late May on one of the big Shannon Lakes in the mid-west of Ireland. The dying sun, fiery orange-red, dropped towards the Clare hills away to the west with an almost biblical radiance. Against the darker background of the hills, adult mayfly could be seen flying erratically out across the lake, dipping to touch the water and rising again as they laid their eggs for species immortality in their final act of life.

All around the lake, small boats nestled into the lee of little islands or merged against the background of the densely wooded shores of every bay and inlet. Anglers sat quietly, occasionally standing, watching for the tell-tale signs of a feeding trout. Now and then the rasping sound of a fly reel signalled that someone was casting to a feeding fish. The muffled sound of quiet conversation drifted across the water and here and there a louder exchange between nearby boats could be heard - *Plenty of gnats dancing in here still; Anything stirring over there?; Hope the wind doesn't shift.* As the sun flared its final farewell to the day along the distant purple hills, the signs were all looking good.

Two friends stood together in their boat and looked along the fifteen-foot wide slick of calm water which ran in a gentle sinuous curve away in front of them. The slick commenced about fifty yards behind them at the rocky tip of Hazel Point and stretched for three miles towards Hare Island, away down the wind on the distant Clare side of the lake. There was a good scattering of flies on the water already and they could see egg-laying females fluttering past them in the balmy evening light.

Behind them in the trees and bushes along the shore, tens of thousands of male mayflies joined in the spectacular dance of the gnats, rising rhythmically on beating transparent wings and falling gently again in the timeless courtship dance performed by their ancient species for three hundred million years. Occasionally an adult female, bigger than the males and with beautiful translucent violet-tinted wings, would dart into the dancing throng to be claimed by a partner. Together they would drop to the grass and then rise again to fly uncertainly towards the waters edge where the male would fall away, spent and dying, onto the water, the female flying on out with her precious eggs. Then, spent and exhausted, she too would drop onto the water to die, her mission in life complete.

The surface of the lake downwind from Hazel Point was strewn with dead and dying females as the two men quietly watched the slick. In the fluffy, wind-riffled water to either side of the slick, the flies were difficult to see, the slight wind-buffeting tending to sink them into the surface film. But in the calm of the slick they could be clearly seen and the two watched and chatted, reassuring each other that they had picked the right spot, read the signs well, and that they would not be better off somewhere else on the twenty-six mile long lake with all its bays and islands. They knew that conditions were near perfect. The slick was ideal: female flies beating out slightly upwind from the shelter of Hazel Point would fall back into the water above the point and drift back towards them and on down the slick towards the Hare. Big trout prefer to feed on gnat quietly and without effort. The calm water of the slick provided the ideal situation for them, the dead and exhausted flies lying motionless on the water, sitting targets for the trout which would simply have to tilt gently back on the tail to sip them down. And the slick would also give the fish a line to feed along, a focus as it were, the trout preferring to move slowly forward as it fed, crossing obliquely over and back across the slick but all the time moving upwind until it reached its territorial limit and turned back again, mopping up the feast of flies.

The two anglers had fished mayfly together for 24 years and they both sensed that this was a special evening; that for an hour or so until the light faded completely, something spectacular could happen. Even if no trout came their way they were enjoying one of the marvelous sights of the lake, a clouding mass of mayfly spinners dancing along the shore as far as the eye could see. Both knew that a decent trout was just a bonus to simply being there. Across the lake an outboard engine coughed into life as somebody succumbed to the urge that faraway hills are greener.

As the tension and excitement grew, the two watched for the signs of a feeding fish. They had a small anchor out to hold the boat on station in the ten-foot deep water. She sat nicely athwart the slick so that both could comfortably watch the water in front and both could cast without obstruction if and when a trout showed. They knew what they were looking for, that most times the rise of even a big fish taking gnats could be so quiet and so easy to miss. Just like a tiny dimple on the water, no more than a rain drop. But every so often there can be a more aggressive rise as a struggling egg-laying female is taken, and often, too, if a fish is feeding really hard and there are a lot of gnats on the water, he will cruise slowly forward, very close below the surface, taking flies with a heart stopping show of head, dorsal fin and tail in almost slow motion.

Suddenly from Michael, a whisper, *I heard something!* Eyes straining, all senses alert. *There, right in front of us!* Thirty yards down the slick, a quiet sipping noise and the tiniest break in the surface film as the trout rose again. As they watched, the fish took another fly eighteen inches right of the first and then another a couple of feet further up the slick. He was feeding well! Then a good show of head, dorsal and - *Lord, so far behind!* - a great leisurely sweeping tail. A big fish, a great fish, feeding quietly and efficiently up toward the anchored boat, unaware, undisturbed, full of confidence.

Two flies in the air, reels rasping as the men worked line out, and down went the two spent gnats onto the slick about eight feet closer to the boat from where he last had shown. Dead right for him, one fly directly between him and the boat and the other a few feet to one side. Wait, be patient. Which way was he travelling, obliquely left or right? Would he take, or even notice, an artificial among so many naturals? Surely he's passed under the fly by now - should I lift and cast again? Has he turned back down the slick or have we put him down, alarmed him somehow? Perhaps he's seen or sensed the boat. Both men reaching forward, ready to react to anything, hearts beating madly, eyes riveted to their own fly. Keep your eye on it or you'll lose it among the mass of naturals, yet try to watch the water around you for that fish. Concentrate! Control your reactions if you do rise him. He's a big fish, be firm but don't hit him too hard or he'll break you! Try to see which way he's moving as he takes. Where is he gone? Cast again; no, leave it, or you might frighten him, put him down. It was less than three seconds since he last rose, but the thoughts and doubts came tumbling fast and furious.

Suddenly one of the flies just seemed to vanish. One moment it was there, the next it was gone! So quiet was the take that unless he had been concentrating precisely on the fly, the fisherman would have seen or heard nothing. The second angler, vastly experienced, watching his own fly a few feet to the right, hoping that the fish was coming his way, on his side of the slick, nerves twitching with excitement, was aware of nothing until he saw in his peripheral vision his crouching friend suddenly straighten up, fly rod rising in his right arm, left arm ripping in slack line as he struck the fish. Saw the line straighten, falling beads of water glistening in the fading light, heard the shriek of the reel as the trout tore wildly away on its first powerful run. Saw a big trout pitch and tumble in a welter of spray and golden flank and heard his friend gasp, almost as in prayer, *Yes, I'm in him*...........

Beginnings

Like most aspects of our development, the process of becoming a fisherman is a result of both inherited body chemistry - our genes - and, of course, opportunity. In both cases, for me, the motivation came from my mother's side of the family. Her father was a bank manager who had always been interested and greatly involved in country life. Mad about fishing, he had first worked in County Limerick and had enjoyed in their heyday, some of the great fisheries of that region, in particular the rivers Deel and Maigue and of course the mighty Shannon itself.

Later he moved to Clonmel, County Tipperary, in the Golden Vale of southern Ireland, and it was here, near the town of Clonmel, that my mother, Clare, was born. She was forever intensely proud of this Tipperary heritage and, even though she came to Dublin in her early twenties to work, her love for, and identity with, Tipperary never diminished.

The area is blessed with some of the most stunningly beautiful countryside in Ireland through which flow some of our finest trout fisheries. The River Suir, the main artery of the region, actually flows through Clonmel, while many of its fine tributaries are within easy reach of the town, even by bicycle. If you had an interest in good trout fishing and were offered your choice of centres in which to live happily ever after, you could do a lot worse than settle for Clonmel.

My mother had a great love for all things connected to the countryside. She could recognise all the different plants and berries, and nothing pleased her more than to spend an hour or two picking blackberries or fraughans or whatever was in season, and producing a tart of exquisite flavours to cover with lashings of fresh cream which she loved to get direct from the creamery. The trip to the creamery, in the company of donkeys towing little swaying carts with their precious churns on board, was a ritual in itself. The thick, golden cream was measured into the flask by the pint by a man who was always smiling and good humoured, and an extra dollop at the end, (just to be sure), would feed a family for a week!

Although she was not a particularly active fisherwoman herself, as a child she could tickle a trout with the best of them, and to her great delight she once caught a fine trout of four and three quarter pounds on Lough Corrib. It took me most of my fishing life to do better than that! She loved to tell stories of the fishing escapades of her father and her brother Jim, and the many colourful characters that they knew along the riverside as she grew up. She knew what a powerful interest fishing was and how it opened windows to so many other aspects of our beautiful land that its value was incalculable. And so it was inevitable that as soon as I showed any enthusiasm for fishing she would encourage me and facilitate me in every possible way, and I owe to her memory a great debt of gratitude for an interest I have enjoyed for a lifetime.

***

Although I was born in Dublin city, I was interested in fish for as far back as I can remember. Wherever we went, I was fascinated by what might be lurking beneath the surface of the water, be it river, lake, pond or sea. As a child I would not cross a bridge without stopping to hang over the parapet, looking for the flicker of a trout or watching for the sign of a rise, trying to convince myself that a swaying frond of weed was really a monster fish. Even in Dublin's city centre I can remember as a small child watching the big grey mullet grazing on the weeds of the Liffey at O'Connell Bridge in the heat of a summer day.

It was always great to get out of the city, even for a day, but a week in the country was sheer heaven for my brother and sister and me. My grandmother and my aunt Betty lived in New Ross in County Wexford, and once or twice a year we used to take the bus down to spend a week's holiday with them. This was always high adventure. Betty was an hilarious character who revelled in life and living and who had an uncanny knack of never seeming to worry about anything. My grandmother, too, was a wonderful, larger than life person, full of tales of the country and a master of mock severity as she tried to chase us youngsters off to our beds at the end of each action-packed day. We always had a brilliant time when we stayed with them, and adventures in the countryside seemed to be everyday events down there.

On those trips to New Ross the city ended and the countryside began at the bus terminus in Dublin. The little red single decker 'country buses' used to depart from the quays along the Liffey opposite the old McBirneys store and to this day I can remember the thrill of standing in the queue as it shuffled along towards the door at the rear of the bus. The long distance passengers always had all sorts of luggage with them and it was amazing to watch the bus swallowing up the huge variety of odds and ends that were destined for far off County Wexford. Suitcases, big brown parcels, hens in baskets, you name it, were carefully stowed on board, and awkward things like bikes and prams were carried up a ladder at the back of the bus and secured in a big roof well. The ultimate excitement came when the queue brought me to a point beside the front wheel, which of course towered over me, and I could smell all the wonderful tarry, rubbery smells that only a bus wheel seemed to generate! As I sniffed the glorious odours, I used to imagine all the magic places that this enormous, friendly wheel had travelled to as it wound its way through Ireland's countryside, but in particular I had visions of sparkling rivers teeming with fish, and of men in tweed jackets, hats studded with trout flies leaning over the bridges and watching the trout splashing in the river below. Then on went the queue, onto the bus we got, and the excitement was almost unbearable as we pulled away, turned left across O'Connell Bridge and then left again back down the far side of the quays towards adventures unlimited.

Although the River Barrow flowed through the town of New Ross it was not a fishing river at this point in its journey to the sea. It was tidal and wide, navigable by quite large coastal vessels which came right up to the town to load and unload their cargoes on great clanking, chattering cranes. Definitely not a play area for little boys. But there was a place where my grandmother used to take us walking which was just heaven. It was a little wood just a mile or so outside New Ross where in the nearby fields we would pick wild mushrooms on evenings in late summer. She showed us how to thread them on a grass stem with a knot tied in it, and we would bring them home to fry in butter, and the flavours were unbelievable. But for me the real magnet of this place was that in the middle of the wood there was a tiny pond, maybe thirty yards across, with a little stream flowing through it, and in it were lots of small, and maybe not so small, trout. I was fascinated by this secret little bower and used to beg to stay on watching the insects weaving and wheeling in the evening sun and the dimpling little rises of the trout. If only I was bigger and I could fish....

***

During the summer of my fifth year I finally did get to fish, though not in New Ross, and I can remember the day as if it were yesterday. My mother had an elderly aunt who lived in Kilkeel, a little fishing port on the coast of County Down, and she and I went up on the train from Dublin to visit the old lady who had been unwell.

The weather was warm and sunny (wasn't it always when we were small!) and on one of the mornings my mother took me down to the harbour to see the fishing trawlers. At the end of the pier I lay on my tummy, my mother clinging tightly to my legs, to look into the water. As I watched I could see these small, mottled little fish with very large heads creeping about on their pectoral fins a few feet below the surface. I learned later that they are called bullheads, but as children we always referred to them as 'cobblers' and I'm sure every child who has ever fished must have caught one in his or her time. "Could we try to catch one", I pleaded, "please!".

We hurried back into the town in the hot sunshine to buy a hook and a 10 yard card of brown linen line. Then back down to the sea where we knocked a couple of limpets off the rocks, and then out again to the end of the pier. Would they still be there? Would they have disappeared with the falling tide? Of course not! There they were, three or four of them, each fully three inches long, still creeping about on their pectoral fins and blending so well with the yellowed stone of the harbour wall that sometimes it was easier to see their dark shadows than to pick out the little fish themselves in the bright sunshine.

My mother, resourceful to a tee, tied a small stone on as a weight, baited the hook with a piece of limpet and I lay on the pier and lowered the bait to one of the cobblers. No interest! I nudged it nearer to him and still no interest. It was an utterly absorbing contest. The little fish and I were alone on the planet! Eventually, to my joy, one of them sidled carefully over and pulled at the bait. I could feel the little jerk as he gave a backward flick to tear it off the hook, but he quickly dropped it again. Back he came, and again, and eventually he took the whole bait and he was hooked! Squealing with excitement I pulled him up the harbour wall and onto the pier where my mother carefully unhooked him and, after a brief moment of admiration, back he went into the water.

I could think of nothing else for weeks afterwards. The capture of the cobbler was definitely a point of no return, a Rubicon of sorts, and from that moment on the most certain thing about my future was that fishing would be a part of it.

***

When I was about five years old we moved from Dublin city and went to live in the little seaside village of Blackrock about six miles south of the city. I went with my mother on the tram to view the house before we rented it, and I can still remember my childlike delight at the profusion of yellow and gold marigolds in the front garden. There weren't too many of these growing outside our flat in the centre of Dublin! It was a wonderful house with three floors and all sorts of lovely old nooks and crannies. But better still there was a huge garden at the back, maybe forty yards long, with a trellis half way down, and lovely lawns between it and the house. Beyond the trellis there were lots of fruit trees and vegetables and, at the bottom of the garden, a high stone wall separated us from the flawless greens and courts of Blackrock bowling and tennis club. Did I like it, my mother asked with a smile, and I could tell from her own expression that she too had fallen head over heels for it! I couldn't wait to get out there.

Sadly we were not there too long before tragedy struck at our family. I was still only seven when my father fell victim to an illness that finally took his life at a cruelly early age. Although his first love had been hurling, then rugby and golf, he had made the odd fishing pilgrimage to the Corrib with some of his friends before his illness, but I was much too young to be brought along on those trips and fate decreed that we would never fish together. I do remember being taken out swimming in the sea by him, riding on his back at Seapoint near Blackrock, when I must have been very young indeed. He was a big man, six foot three, very powerfully built, and it was like sitting on a whale! The water seemed to me to be unfathomably deep and, as I clung like a leech to his neck, I felt that if I slipped off I would sink beneath the waves and never be heard of again!

During his illness my mother was completely devoted to trying to look after him, first of all at home and later when he was in hospital. Having no car, she used the tram to get in to the hospital in Dublin or, as was often the case, she would get a lift from friends. My sister and brother and I visited him regularly. I'm sure we were told, gently and over time, how serious his illness was. But somehow the finality of it didn't register, certainly with me, until one glorious summer's day in June I was called out of class in the National school by a very subdued and sombre head mistress. My mother's sister, Mabel, herself so young, hugged me and told me with great tenderness that my father had passed away. I could not comprehend the finality of it. Later, the tears of my mother made it real.

***

My mother was a wonderful craftswoman and now, with three young children to rear on her own, she took to sewing to make ends meet. Somehow, through her determination, we got by. She must have worked so hard and managed her affairs so well to get us through those times, and I don't remember ever feeling that we were short of anything. But how she managed to get me a bike for my ninth birthday was, in hindsight, truly a miracle!

On the morning of my birthday I was told that a surprise would be coming by car at a certain time and of course the excitement was almost unbearable. By *car!* What could it be that had to be brought by car? Having an August birthday I had the luxury of always being free of school for that day of day's, and long before the appointed hour I was fiddling and twitching at the gate, waiting for the sight of a car (a rare enough sight) to turn into our road. At last I saw a car belonging to a friend of my mother's coming up the hill, horn beeping, to pull into the kerb outside our house.

I could not believe what I saw. The bike was a brand new Phillips, lustrous black and gleaming chrome, and as the handlebars and pedals were tightened into place I couldn't wait for my maiden voyage. There were very few cars about in those early post war days and our road was perfect for a learner and, with a steadying adult hand on the saddle, I was soon getting the hang of it with scarcely a scuffed knee!

***

It wasn't long before I was pretty good on the bike and began riding it to school. And once my mother was happy that I was safe on it, I was given the all clear to cycle off with a couple of slightly older boys on fishing trips. One of these, Val, became a lifelong friend of mine with whom I shared many's a great fishing adventure. Our favourite destination then was a little stream about 5 miles south of Blackrock, near what was then the country village of Loughlinstown. The stream passed under the main Dublin to Bray road near the Silver Tassie pub and reached another bridge on the road from Killiney to Shankill, where we used to leave our bikes. Here it flowed through some woodland before meandering through a couple of fields to pass under a railway bridge and over a shingly bar on the shore, and into the sea.

It was a beautiful clear stream and had lots of small darting trout in every nook and cranny, particularly in the wooded area. We regarded these trout under the trees as superior and sophisticated creatures, much too difficult for us to catch with all those bushes and trees about. But further downstream, as the river meandered through the open fields, there were fewer trout but lots of eels that were much easier to catch, and very acceptable targets for us.

My older pals had proper fishing rods at this stage and I had a hand line and some hooks and a tin of worms, and I was as happy as a sandboy. We caught eels and the occasional small trout, always on worms, but the ultimate prize of a trout caught on a fly eluded us. Until one memorable day Val tried once again to fish a fly close to the wooded area and this time, success! A lovely little brook trout took the fly. John and I were delighted for him and the three of us must have spent about half an hour admiring every speckle on the fish before we saddled up and pedalled like mad for home to show him off.

First stop was Val's house where we showed the trout to his proud mum and it was placed with appropriate reverence on a plate and locked into the safety of the larder, away from the family cat. Then on to my place to tell my mother the news. Eventually, after hearing every last detail of the catch, my mum, as always, asked Val would he like to stay to tea, and I can still see his chest swelling with pride as he said no thank you, that he was going home to have his trout! Now that was *real* fishing!

***

Also well within bike range was Dun Laoghaire harbour. We used to cycle down to the end of the west pier and join the other small boys; fishing for pouting or little pollack off the steps leading down to the water, laughing and squabbling like a flock of starlings on a lawn.

Here we would watch in silent awe as the adult anglers assembled big powerful rods and exotic fixed-spool reels. They would bait up with 'rag' or 'lug', big marine worms that they had dug up on the shore, and then rock the weight to and

21

fro for maximum momentum before slinging the gear out, almost half way to Wales it seemed! Then the bale arm clicked back as the handle turned and we would watch the smooth in and out movement of the spool as the slack was taken up while the angler cocked his head from side to side, visualising, we felt, every single thing that was happening out there in the deep around his apparatus of wire and hook. Truth to tell, most of them used the old Nottingham wooden reels, but the fixed spools were the ones that interested us. We would keep an eye on these real anglers while we fished away at the steps, and we'd all rush over to the wall, whooping with joy, each time a glistening mackerel was reeled up the harbour wall.

***

As a family in those days we often used to walk down to the sea at Blackrock where we kids would have a wonderful time, in and out of the sea, while the mothers chatted and relaxed in the sunshine. We had all sorts of things to do. Sometimes we would idle away the hours collecting pieces of sea-worn coloured glass to see who could get the most varieties. If the tide were out, we would spend hours looking for crabs in the crevices of the seaweed covered rocks and often get our fingers nipped in the process. And when the tide was in, we would fish for crabs from the 'Slanty Rock', a favourite spot just over the sea wall from the pedestrian bridge that crossed the railway line. A length of string, a stone for a weight, and a limpet or mussel tied to the end was all you needed. Just drop it into the water and wait for a few minutes before pulling it carefully back so that any interested crab that had taken hold of it in his claws would not let go with the sudden movement. The competition was fierce to see who could catch the biggest or the most crabs in the afternoon, and all were returned unharmed from our 'holding pool' at the end of the day.

Sometimes at low tide we would be asked by a friendly fisherman to help him catch 'peelers'. These were soft-backed crabs that had shed their shells and were in the process of growing a new one. Our pal told us that they were a deadly bait for bass and codling and other exotic fish, and we would listen, wide eyed, as he told us about the monsters he and his pals reeled in through the surf and waves of far off Greystones beach. We were delighted to help search for peelers and he would pay us a hal'penny each for any that we found. This was serious spending money in those days. You could get a nice toffee bar for a penny, or six 'honey bee' toffee sweets, and it gave us the opportunity to innocently ask the old lady in the sweet shop on Georges Avenue, "How much are the penny toffees?", and wait for her to chase us out onto the street with a sweeping brush in mock indignation. She was a dear, and our best friend again an hour later!

The railway station was right beside our play area at the beach, and the track ran along the seashore from Ringsend in Dublin all the way to Dun Laoghaire and far away to the south to places we had never seen. We could see the trains coming from the Dublin side for several miles away across the curve of the bay, the puffs of white smoke and steam contrasting like little cumulus clouds against the blue of the summer sky. As the train pulled into Blackrock station we would already have run up onto the pedestrian footbridge that crossed the track at the end of the platform and we would eagerly wait for the guard to wave his flag and blow his whistle. The clanking, puffing monster would start forward and we would stand, full of bravado, and watch as it came straight towards us on the track below, jumping into the centre of the tiny bridge at the last minute as our world was engulfed in a huge belch of the sweetest smelling smoke and soot and grime imaginable. Heaven was a blast from a steam train!

***

On rainy Saturday afternoons, if we had 'been good', we would be given the money to go to the 'flicks' in the Regent Cinema in Blackrock. This was a great treat! We would queue, it seemed for hours, before the doors opened and what was known as the 'fourpenny rush' for the cheap seats near the screen began. The better seats, costing a whole ten pence each, were further back away from us lot, separated by an aisle where the glamorous usherette used to stand at the interval with a tray of sweets and ice cream far beyond our meagre resources! During any distractions the more daring among us would dart back from the fourpennies to cower in a tenpenny seat and hope that the move hadn't been observed. Because if it was, woe betide you, as Peter, the huge and forbidding head usher, would unerringly sweep down on the unfortunate and fix the wretch, like a weasel would a rabbit, in the beam of his huge torch before either returning him, minus his dignity, to his fourpenny seat or, on a really bad day, ejecting him out onto the street altogether.

The 'flicks' were great, always either Cowboys and Indians, Tarzan of the Apes, or gangster movies, and the leading man was always known in Dublinese as 'The Chap' and his beautiful girl 'The Mot'. We were always up for the Chap of course, and the shrieks and cheers as he rescued the Mot from some diabolical disaster would have been heard in the next parish. In addition to the main film there would usually be an episode of a serial. These 'folly-ups', as they were affectionately known, might run for four or five weeks and I am absolutely certain that none of us ever saw one of them in its entirety.

***

By the end of my tenth year there was no doubt in anyone's mind that I was destined to be an angler. My mother, in particular, knew that this was not just a passing interest and somehow for my next birthday she managed to get me a fly rod and a little Bakelite reel. What sacrifices she must have made to manage to afford these. The rod was a beauty, split cane, and ideal for either fly or worm fishing, and of course I was ecstatic and couldn't wait to try it out. But first I had to get some flies and I went with my brother into Dublin on the bus, to the old Stream and Field tackle shop on Pearse Street, where a half dozen wet flies were carefully selected with the friendly advice of the two brothers who used to run the shop.

The lovely old shop, filled with fantastic fishing and shooting gear of every imaginable sort is gone now, and Dublin much the poorer for its absence.

***

My birthday being in August, the trout year was getting late by now, and although we did make a few trips to Loughlinstown before the last day of September saw the end of the trout fishing for that year, the christening of the rod had to wait for another season.

First Trout

During that autumn and winter I discovered the infinite delights of the local libraries and started to devour every book I could find on angling, whether coarse or game, salt or fresh water. I became familiar with the names of all the popular tyings of trout flies and eagerly read about the great trout fisheries of the world, from the chalk streams of England to Lake Taupo in far off New Zealand. Through the pages I fished for monster pike in the wilds of the west of Ireland and stalked the wily carp at dawn among the lily pads of secluded ponds in England. I was in my element.

My mother married again and not only did my stepfather, Claude, have a car but he was also very interested in the countryside and loved driving us for picnics to parts of Wicklow which were far beyond the reach of our bikes. An added bonus for me was that he too was very fond of fishing, which meant that the trips for our new extended family almost always took us close to a river or a lake.

When March arrived, the bicycles once again headed for the little river at Loughlinstown, fly rods tied to cross bars and lunch boxes clamped to back carriers. We parked our bikes at the little bridge and the three of us started to put our tackle together. I had practised lots of different knots during the winter, with the help of the many library books, and I had no trouble tying cast to line and Greenswell Glory onto the cast. One fly was enough, particularly as we were now bravely trying to fish along the wooded part of the river where we knew that there were more trout but the danger of snagging on bushes or trees was great.

On that first trip we had caught nothing before lunch but, after a break for sandwiches and flasks of hot tea, we started again, full of renewed optimism. I can still remember standing in my wellies in a little shallows with the line trailing downstream, idly watching Val who was fishing about thirty yards above me. Suddenly I felt a sharp tug on the line and, whirling around in surprise, I saw a trout splashing and skittering on the surface downstream of me. I could feel every movement through the little rod and John, a few yards upstream, whooped with delight as I started to reel the fish towards me. My heart was pounding for fear of losing him at any stage but lady luck was smiling brightly on me that March afternoon and I lifted the little fish, in all its spotted resplendence, onto the grassy verge.

My first trout on the fly! My two companions were at my side in a flash, congratulating me and admiring the little fish that we quickly despatched and laid on the grass. Every speckle and spot was commented on before he was carefully rolled up in wet grass and popped into the little tool bag that hung from the saddle of my bike! Based on my recollections of how I felt at that time, this was quite a fish. But when I realise that, wrapped in grass, he still managed to fit in that little saddle-bag, well.....

Nevertheless he was mine, all my own work, and I pedalled furiously all the way home to show him off. I must have stopped five or six times during the journey to check the saddlebag and make sure that the little trout was still there. Needless to say my tea that evening was going to be trout and I often laughingly think that it must have been a little trout like that, which spawned the Irish infamous expression, 'Sure wouldn't he be grand with a rasher!'

***

27

My folks decided to take us caravanning for the Easter weekend to the Glen of Aherlow in County Tipperary. This beautiful valley, in the shadow of the Galtee Mountains, is one of the loveliest places in the country. Through its lush meadows the River Aherlow flows to meet the majestic River Suir near the ancient town of Cahir some six or seven miles to the east. In those days there were really no restrictions on where you parked your caravan as long as you had permission and you were not causing a traffic hazard, and of course nothing remained behind you when you left, except the proverbial footprints. We parked the caravan at Tankardstown bridge, so close to the river that you could almost have fished out of the window.

The first thing I wanted to do was to get to the river so out came the rod and flies and down I went to try my luck. Although I could see fish rising here and there, I couldn't stir a fin, but there was no doubt that this was a really good trout stream and I felt that I was in there with a great chance of catching something.

That evening after dark we were all sitting in the caravan reading and chatting when there was a tap on the door. It was a priest, who introduced himself to us as Father John Hayes, parish priest of Bansha, whose focal point was the village of the same name a few miles up the road. My mother immediately recognised him to be a very famous man indeed, founder of an organisation called Muintir na Tire, the "People of the Land", a wonderfully successfully co-operative movement to develop the cultural, economic and social aspects of Irish rural life. He was a small, very likeable man, later to become a canon, and he was delighted at the offer of a cup of tea and the chance to chat for a while.

We talked of many things, particularly my mother's Tipperary roots, which he was suitably impressed with, and later on he was very interested to hear that I was mad about fishing. He looked approvingly at the flies in my box and reassured me that the fishing was very good at the moment and that I should definitely have some luck if I concentrated on the right places. As he shook hands to leave, he winked at me and said, 'Remember to fish the rapids'.

The following morning I was down to the river immediately after breakfast, remembering what Father Hayes had said. Fish the rapids. I looked down towards the tail of a pool to where the river narrowed into a fast and shallow run for about fifty yards, rocks showing here and there in the broken water, before it opened out again into another gentle glide. Could this be what he meant? Could trout actually survive in that fast, shallow water? Why would they want to live there, having to work so hard in that strong current? I moved down to the top of the run and started to cast the flies. Within a few minutes I felt a tug and saw a splash in the water below me. I had risen one. I fished on, rising two more fish, until I reached the bottom of the run. Then I reeled up and walked straight on downstream to the next fast stretch, passing all the slower water that I had been concentrating on yesterday. Within a few minutes I rose another, and this time, joy of joys, he stayed with me. He fought like a demon in the fast water, but he was mine, and to crown a great afternoon I caught two more in the streams and shallows before I wandered happily back to the caravan thanking God, Father John and my parents for bringing me to this fabulous spot. An important lesson had been learned. Wet flies, fast water!

***

The following morning my brother Dick and I stole quietly out of the caravan at about 7.00 a.m. while the others were still fast asleep. It was a beautiful, sunny morning and we climbed down the little wooden stile to the riverbank and walked quietly upstream through the sweet smelling dewy grass, just watching. I had read in the library books of some rivers holding really good trout, two or three pounds or more, but I had never actually seen such fish and in my mind I imagined that they were only to be found in the Test or the Itchen or the other famous chalk streams of southern England where only the very wealthy could fish. I had been quite content to see the little half pounders as I leant across Tankardstown bridge and peered into the sun-dappled, pebbly shallows of the Aherlow.

We reached a quiet, sheltered stretch of the river where the early morning sun filtered through lots of bushes and, hiding in the long grass, crept closer to the waterside to look. When our eyes became accustomed to the scene I noticed an unusual sort of pulsing movement quite close to us in the river and looking harder, I made out the shape of a terrific trout, the moving mouth and gills of which had first attracted my attention. I nudged Dick in the arm, nodded towards the fish and he saw it straight away. Spellbound we watched, able to make out the big red and orange spots on his flanks, the easy movement of his tail and pectoral fins as he held his position, and the occasional effortless sideways movement as he inspected something passing him by in the water. He must have weighed at least two pounds, maybe more. And, knowing now what to look for, we saw other big trout as we crept quietly up the river, edging carefully over to the bank to peep through the grass into the water. It was a marvellously exciting couple of hours for my brother and me. Not another soul in sight, just us and the trout and the fat, contented Tipperary cattle standing knee-deep tails swishing, in the sweetest grass in all the world.

***

Visits to far off places like the Glen of Aherlow were as rare as the place itself and most of our trout fishing encounters occurred in the beautiful county of Wicklow, the Garden of Ireland itself. From the sparkling sand dunes of Brittas Bay to the monastic solitude of Glendalough, from the rugged peaks of Lugnaquilla to the gentle Vale of Avoca, Wicklow has it all. In the early 1950's cars were still fairly scarce and, even though these places are relatively close to Dublin, they were always uncrowded. The only public transport that visited Glendalough was the old Saint Kevin's bus that ground its way up the steep slope of Calary Hill carrying its happy complement of hill walkers, mountaineers, fishermen and other lovers of the countryside bound for some of the most beautiful parts of Ireland. This privately owned bus was a godsend to so many people who had no other way of reaching the places they loved so much.

We were very lucky to have the car and whenever we went off somewhere for the day I would bring along my fishing rod. And, whether by accident or design (I suspect my mother had a hand in it), most of the places we did go to, like Laragh, Rathdrum or Roundwood, had a river or a lake close by.

And they were such wonderful places. I have a picture in my mind of lying among the springy heather, watching two ravens wheeling and stalling in a clear blue sky, softly 'kronking' to each other in the utter stillness of a summer's day. Five hundred feet below me, at the foot of the scarp, a silver-blue stream meanders down a green, boulder strewn valley. Across the valley, on the far side of Lough Tay, the ground rises again into the chaotic, frost-shattered scree slope of Duff Mountain. It is a wilderness area that can take your breath away. Ireland's Montana on Dublin's very doorstep.

Lough Dan and Lough Tay, and the beautiful Annamoe River that joins them, were perhaps the most popular places for us to go. You could get to Lough Dan by road from

Roundwood village and fish from the shore, or hire a boat for five shillings for the day. The lake is very deep, and food is scarce, except for the big ferox trout that supposedly lived in the deeps and plundered the dashing little trout that searched for the occasional fly in the upper layers. A Coch-y-bondhu fished dry almost always attracted a trout or two but it didn't matter a bit if you never saw a rise, it was more than enough just to be there, sitting in the boat and surrounded on all sides by the towering mountains of Wicklow. Even though you were out in the lake, the mountains were so dominant, producing an almost claustrophobic feeling like sitting in a gigantic amphitheatre of rare and spectacular beauty. If you ever felt God was close by, it would be here.

You could, on the other hand, leave the car at Luggala, near Sallygap, and walk for three breathtaking miles down the mountain track to where the Annamoe flows into Lough Dan across a beach of purest golden sand. On this little river, which is only about two miles long, I learnt many things. Not only about fish and fishing but also about wildlife in general. The water was clean and peaty and the dashing wild trout were dark and handsome with golden bellies and vivid red and black spots. There was always something spectacular to see. Kestrels hovering in the clear blue sky, buzzards soaring in the thermal currents between the mountains, the screech and flash of white and blue as a jay dashed for cover in the forested sections, dippers and kingfishers on the river, and the air full of the bubbling, sweet sound of larks.

There were bigger creatures too. Foxes, badgers, hares, rabbits and even otters, were regular sights. I had the most wonderful twenty minutes one afternoon, watching four otter cubs playing around a pinnacle-shaped granite boulder that stuck about two feet out of the centre of the river. They were having fantastic fun clambering up onto the rock and sliding down into the water, tissing and yikkering to each other like children in a playground, until a parent obviously sensed my presence and whistled them off. In unison they swam silently across to a steep overhang on the other side of the river and just disappeared. Although I waited hopefully in the long grass for fifteen or twenty minutes they never came back.

As an added bonus, the geology of this part of Wicklow is totally fascinating with its granite and quartzite mountains, wild scree slopes, and magnificent valleys, rivers and waterfalls. The last ice age has overprinted everything with an incredible suite of additional features that defy the imagination. Great ice hewn cauldrons are now deep (we kids thought bottomless!) lakes like Lough Tay, while the inexorable movement of massive glaciers tore the craggy spurs from the sides of the old river valleys to produce the classical 'U'-shape of a glacial valley like that of the Annamoe itself. The ubiquitous rock outcrops, scratched and scraped by the passing ice, still preserve, after tens of thousands of years, the striations that show the direction of movement of the great sheets of ice that once entombed the entire area. When the ice finally melted, only ten thousand years ago, it left behind a lifeless wilderness, with no plants, no animals, no freshwater fish. Gradually, as temperatures slowly rose, the creatures and plants that now inhabit our country, including our own ancestors, slowly made their way here from southern Europe until the melting ice water raised sea levels and cut us off from Britain and the Continent to leave us forever an island.

It was in this wild and fascinating landscape of Wicklow that I first became interested in geology, little realising that one day I would be fortunate enough to have this incredible subject become my way of life.

***

Another favourite spot to visit was a little valley of the Avonmore River that originates at Glendalough and flows into the Vale of Avoca, joining the Avonbeg at the beautiful 'Meeting of the Waters'. In a secluded little vale not far from the village of Laragh, an old stone bridge spans a gorgeous stretch of the river, with on one side some old cottages and on the other a small church. Upstream of the bridge there are some nice little runs which were grand for wet fly fishing, and some deep eddying pools where we used to fish for trout with worms when the water was high and coloured. Below the bridge, the river cascades through a forested gorge in a series of white rapids, a totally unfishable torrent of raging water and huge granite boulders.

One day, I must have been about 11 years old, we were half way to this beautiful place for a family picnic, when to my consternation I realized that I had left my fishing reel behind. I can still remember the sense of hopelessness as my mother told me not to worry, that we would think of something, and I would get to fish!

When we got to Avondale and parked the car, all the rest of the family started to carry the picnic gear to our favourite spot by the water's edge while I surveyed the river in abject dismay. Nobody else had any fishing tackle with them so I couldn't even borrow a length of line. The day was a disaster, but rescue was at hand. My mother had swiftly disappeared as soon as the car had stopped and now, about ten minutes later, she came back with a big smile on her face holding out a grand reel to me and asking would this do? Characteristically, she had knocked on the door of a complete stranger and explained the situation to the lady of the house, who was only too delighted to lend her son's fishing reel for the afternoon. Not only did I have my days fishing but the two ladies became good friends and my mother always dropped in for a cup of tea and some scones whenever we went there again.

Did I ever thank her enough for all the things she did for me?

***

Later that Summer I had a brush with paradise on an evening that I still think about in great detail and know that I will never forget! It was mid June, the last day of the school year, and when I got home in the afternoon after finishing the last exams, my folks asked would I like, 'as a reward', to go fishing for the evening. It was a magnificent mid-summer's evening as we set out, warm and sunny, with the added inner glow of no more school for weeks to come. We parked the car at a deserted Lugalla and started down the mountain path towards Lough Dan. I have always loved that time of year when everything is so brand new and green, and this evening seemed especially brilliant. The gorse blazed yellow everywhere and the little river Annamoe looked like a thin blue ribbon below us in the valley.

As we reached the bottom of the pass and walked through the granite boulders across a field to the river I had a feeling that this was going to be something really special. I fitted the little split cane rod together and put up two wet flies with more than the usual anticipation. I can't remember what they were, probably my old reliable Greenwells Glory was one of them, and I lost myself in the magic of the river. I might as well have been alone in the world. Just me and the mountain sheep and lambs and the singing birds; and the river with its chattering little runs and gentle glides and splashing, rising trout.

I fished down along the streams and runs, casting the two wet flies and twitching them invitingly back across the stream, waiting for a certain rise. I could see many dimples and rings of rising trout in the stiller water but I knew, or felt I knew, that the faster streamy water was best for this wet fly fishing, giving more life to the fly. For an hour or so I continued, seeing trout rising all the time, until I knew beyond doubt that I had the wrong fly up. By now the sun had gone behind the mass of hills on the other side of the valley leaving my quiet world bathed in the almost tangible luminescence of a summer's night when darkness never falls. I reeled in and sat down on a granite boulder, pulled out my little box of flies and studied them carefully. One, a Red Spinner, took my fancy. Spinners were egg layers, eggs were laid in the evening, and maybe that was what the trout were taking. I snipped off the tail fly, tied the Red Spinner on and continued casting and moving down the stream. As I reached the tail of a little run I felt a pluck and saw a swirl in the water below me. At last I was in business and quickly landed a game little trout to break the duck. The Red Spinner had done it.

The next hour passed so quickly. I lost track of everything but the river and the trout, and before I reached the quiet, sandy meanders where the river enters the lake, I had caught four in all and had risen, tumbled and missed ten or twelve more. The action had been almost non stop and the little Red Spinner, almost chewed off the hook, was a tattered and battered looking sight in the half light.

Too soon I heard my name being called from through the trees. *Time to go!* I knew that it was late, it was an hour's walk back up the mountain track to the car and another hour to drive home, but it was desperately hard to leave. The wraith-like wisps of summer night's fog were collecting in little pockets along the river, imparting an almost ghostly atmosphere to the place. I could hear the sheep and their lambs across the river, lost among the scattered mass of granite boulders. An owl hooted from the trees behind me, from where my folks waited patiently for me. As I skipped across the little rocky field towards the trees I couldn't wait to show them the four beautiful little trout in my bag, and I knew with an absolute certainty that I was the luckiest, most privileged youngster in the entire world.

***

The summer passed with trips to the river on the bike and a family holiday in Dunmore East which included a plethora of wonderful sea fishing adventures. Then, reluctantly, back to school in September and finally the deep mid-winter and Christmas time again.

Being twelve I no longer believed in Santa Claus but that didn't (and still doesn't!) reduce the pleasure of exchanging Christmas presents. As a family we always followed the tradition of leaving the presents underneath the Christmas tree to be opened in a blitz of excitement on Christmas morning, and this was always a very special time.

That Christmas among all the parcels under the tree there was a particularly interesting looking one with my name on the gift tag. It was about five inches square, and felt quite substantial. I had no idea what it might be. Although I didn't notice, I'm sure that my mother must have watched me opening it. Inside the cheerful Christmas paper was a brown cardboard box, and inside that, something delicately wrapped in tissue paper. I gently unwrapped the tissue paper and there to my surprise and exquisite delight was a silver fixed spool reel. Hardly believing my good fortune, I took it carefully out of its box, screwed the black handle into its slot, and grinned with joy as the spool moved in and out on its spindle. That little reel, made of aluminium, was and is the Christmas present that I remember and treasure above all others, before or since. I think my mother was as delighted to give it to me as she would have seen I was to receive it.

When *Stream and Field* reopened again after the Christmas holiday I bought myself a small devon minnow and cycled out to Loughlinstown to try the reel out. I can remember standing on the bank of the river, casting the devon out and reeling it back, flashing realistically through the lifeless water, until my freezing hands and feet could take no more and I pedalled homeward again with my precious reel, as fast as I could to warm my petrified body up again.

The Waters of Lilliput

I had searched for it for two whole days. The little three-acre pond gleamed in the early April sunshine like a pot of gold at the end of a rainbow. I sat on my bike, feet on the ground, and stared at it as though it were a mirage which might suddenly disappear again at any moment.

Everywhere I looked I could see the small rings of feeding fish. On the far side, there was a tiny islet connected to the bank by an old fallen tree and close to its bushy shore there was a good solid boil which was surely the take of a decent trout.

It was the last day of the Easter school holiday, not the most opportune time to discover a little paradise, but at least I knew now where it was.

Three days earlier while my pal Ruaidhrí and I were fishing the little river near Loughlinstown, we had met another youngster who was mooching along throwing sticks for his dog to chase. During the course of chatting he asked had we ever fished in the pond at Ballycorus. We shook our heads, and he told us about this hidden pond that was simply alive with fish. He wasn't sure what sort of fish they were, but they were definitely not trout. He was not a fisherman himself but the friend he had been with that day caught about ten of them and put them all back. They were about ten inches long, he gestured with his index fingers, and had lovely yellow fins and big scales. His pal had been fishing with a float and using bread as bait, he remembered. This had been a few years before and he couldn't quite recall the exact location of the pond but thought it was somewhere near Ballycorus, which was not very far from the Loughlinstown river, up towards the Dublin mountains, a couple of miles at most. He remembered having to cycle up a very steep hill to get to it.

Ruaidhrí and I were very interested in this and decided to find the place. During the previous winter I had started reading the *Angling Times* every week and I was fascinated by the articles on coarse fishing, particularly about pike and carp. Richard Walker and other famous English anglers of the day had started to concentrate on big carp in an organised and scientific way. Carp records were tumbling quite regularly, culminating in Walker's huge 44lb fish from Redmire Lake, such a fantastic fish that it was named Clarissa and sent to London Zoo, where it lived for years. Their descriptions of early morning, and even all-night fishing adventures, were exciting and intriguing and I could almost imagine myself there with them in the swirling mists of dawn, watching the silver paper on the line creep eerily forward to indicate a giant carp had taken the bait. In my enthusiasm I had written to Richard Walker for information about carp fishing here in Ireland and I received a very warm and friendly hand written letter back from him telling me about Irish carp waters and giving me the name of a person in Kildare to contact if I was interested. I never got around to making this contact but it was so nice of him to take the time to write back to a complete stranger when there was obviously so much else for him to do. I was very impressed.

Pike, too, had always been a fascination of mine and I had read lots of library books on pike fishing and general pike lore and legends. There was no doubt that pike were the undisputed Jaws of fresh water, the masters of mystique, and it was intriguing to read about the preserved heads of monster pike and the speculation and estimation of what the fish must have weighed in life. Stories of disappearing ducks, cygnets and even dogs, all added to the mythology and the general theme was that out there, in the big lakes of Ireland in particular, there lurked *huge* pike the likes of which had never been captured before. In later years I had great fun with my own children over breakfast on Saturday mornings, serialising for them the imaginary tale of the 'Giant Pike of Ilaunagore'. The central character was of course a monster pike that inhabited a reedy little bay of Lough Derg, and each episode ended with a sinister event like a pet dog or a group of playful cygnets straying too near his lair! There were always squeals of dismay as an episode finished just as the excitement reached fever pitch - and the following Saturday morning the four eager faces, spoons hovering over the Corn Flakes, waited for the saga to continue.

On that first afternoon that the Ballycorus pond was discovered, I watched for about half an hour as little shoals of what I assumed to be rudd dimpled the surface all around. The pond was almost square, with the little island midway along one side, and the banks were quite steep and about 4 or 5 feet high. The shallows at the base of the high banks had that lovely sweet smell of marsh marigolds and pond mud.

There was a profusion of bird life in and around the pond. A heron had flapped noisily out of the islet as I pulled up on my bike. Comical looking coots with their white bills chased each other across the surface in frantic paddling, flapping runs. Two moorhens fussed around the outer margins of the thick beds of irises, trying to ignore the bad manners of their less composed relatives, and in the air, the first swallows of the summer swooped and dipped exultantly, backs gleaming steely-blue in the bright sunshine.

I had my wellies with me and as I squelched along the water line there was an overpowering aura of *fish* about the place. There was a little disused sluice at one end with water cress and celandine growing in the crystal clear water bickering through it. Everywhere there was the sound and sight of insects. I loved the place instantly, and it was with a feeling of reluctance that I finally climbed onto my bike and pedalled off for home, determined to be back at the first opportunity.

***

All that week at school Ruaidhrí and I had planned our first fishing trip to the pond. We made sure we had light nylon on our spinning reels, that we had some small hooks and some split shot, and we acquired a few 'bubble floats from the local tackle shop. We borrowed two or three books on coarse fishing from the library and read all we could on rudd and roach fishing.

In those days we had school on Saturday mornings so it was about 2pm before we finally set off on our bikes on the 5 mile cycle. If anything the pond looked even better, probably because we had fishing gear with us this time. There was nobody else around as we parked our bikes, just the two of us in this secret little heaven of our own. Around the reed and lily beds, dimples and small swirls indicated that the fish were on the move and with trembling fingers we set up our rods, threaded the nylon through the rings and tied on the bubbles and the hooks before squeezing on a few pieces of split shot with our teeth.

We selected a place where there seemed to be lots of activity and as we watched we could see the odd flash of gold as a fish turned sideways in the water. We baited up with small flakes of bread crust, cast towards the shoal, and settled down to see what, if anything, would happen.

Within about ten minutes one of the bubbles twitched invitingly and then slid sideways towards the reeds. Up came the point of a rod and a small boy's face nearly fell in two with delight as the tip of the rod bent into the fish.

That first fish was examined and admired comprehensively and we knew straight away from the pictures and descriptions in the library books that it was indeed a rudd. We had an action-packed afternoon catching about half a dozen each and returning them carefully unharmed to the water, watching as they sped back to rejoin the shoal.

As six o'clock came we couldn't believe where the time had gone and we had to start packing up. Sandwiches and flasks of tea had been wolfed while we fished rather than wasting valuable time and there could hardly have been two happier lads in the world as we cycled homeward. It had been really brilliant and we were determined to go again at the next opportunity.

***

For two or three years we interspersed visits to the pond with our trout fishing escapades. There was no closed season for coarse fishing in Ireland in those days and we visited the pond at all times of the year, from high summer to the darkest depths of winter. On one bitter January day we had to break the ice along one side of the pond to fish, but fish we did.

The great thing about Ballycorus was that we almost always caught something, except on the ice-breaking day. There is nothing more guaranteed to hold a youngster's attention than a measure of success. The rudd were plentiful and a nice size, up to about three quarters of a pound, with the odd slightly bigger one, and we learned, too, the way to handle the fish carefully and to see that they got safely back to their shoal. It was a perfect training ground for us.

***

It was very rare to see anyone else coming to the pond to fish. Only once or twice can I remember a couple of other boys arriving on bikes, and they were quiet and well behaved, interested, like we were, in the fishing. However one memorable summer afternoon a man of about twenty five arrived on a motor bike and nodded a friendly hello to us as he made his way with rod and bag to the far side of the pond, near to the little island. We watched with interest as he set up a spinning rod and started casting a shimmering lure out along the edge of the island and working it back slowly to where he stood, almost waist deep among the irises. Now and again the spinner would catch in the weed and he would raise the rod tip expectantly before pulling it clear. We watched closely, impressed with his skill in flicking the little lure out with such accuracy to within a few feet of the island.

All of a sudden the rod bucked as though he was caught in the weeds again, but this time the man struck hard and almost simultaneously a big trout flung itself two or three times out of the water by the side of the little island. As the trout ran hard for the weed bed the man quickly released some of the tension on the reel and started to play the fish, walking sideways along the waters edge to get some distance away from the dangers of the island.

Of course we dropped everything and ran around to watch the battle. The rod he was using was very light and there was an incredible bend in it as the fish tore through the weeds and twisted and turned like a mad thing. The commotion in the normally quiet pond was spectacular. We lived every moment of the battle as the fish plunged in and out of flaggers and lilies, rod tip thumping with every shake of his head. The man kept quite calm and chatted away to us, giving us a running commentary on the trout's intentions, and his own tactical response to each new danger. After a nail biting eternity the fish tired and he steered it through a gap in the reeds, asking us to bring him his net that he had left on the bank back where he had hooked the fish. We scampered to get it, delighted to be asked to help in such a moment of drama! We could see the trout quite clearly in the water at this stage and it looked really deep and big and powerful with its golden belly and red and orange spots. As he dipped the net in the water the trout made one last rush towards the tangle of weed to his right. We watched, mouths open, as he dropped the net and grabbed the handle of the reel again, while the little rod bent double with the strain of keeping the fish away from catastrophe. Back came the trout, splashing heavily in the shallower water until, with head up, it slid over the net to be lifted out onto the bank.

We watched as he took a small 'priest' out of his bag, quickly knocked it on the head, and released his blue and silver devon. He lay the fish out on some wet lily leaves and we inspected it carefully before eventually it was slipped into the bag. It was a magnificent trout that our new hero reckoned to be about three pounds weight. It was quite the most impressive fish we had ever seen, short and strong, with a huge and powerful spade-like tail.

Our new pal showed us the rod, the reel and the one-inch blue and silver devon he was using. He showed us the anti-kink swivel fitted about three feet above the devon and explained the need for it. And he showed us the slipknot he used and explained the importance of wetting the nylon before tightening the knot. As we hung on his every word, he told us that there were a few big trout in the pond and that, although difficult to catch, they could occasionally be tempted by a spinner, or even on a fly. Then he demonstrated how to cast the minnow with a little flick of his wrist, and we watched as it spun through the air to land with a tiny splash about two feet from the tangled growth at the edge of the island. Then he packed up all his gear, wished us good luck, and off he went on his motor bike along the grassy path, giving us a final wave as he disappeared out of sight onto the tarred road.

Ruaidhrí and I looked at each other and shook our heads in astonishment! Although we had seen the odd rise and the occasional swirl of what clearly was a bigger fish than the rudd, we had never imagined that there was anything out there in our little pond like that big trout!

Afterwards, although we still fished with great enthusiasm for the rudd, we looked through different eyes at the stillness of the pond. Whenever we did see a trout-like rise we watched carefully to see did he come again. If he did, we would try to see what he was taking. We each bought a blue and silver devon but neither of us ever hooked a trout, although it wasn't for want of trying.

***

The few years fishing on the Ballycorus pond were a real joy. Although we had continued to fish the rivers of Wicklow, and our Loughlinstown stream, for trout during the same time, we dearly loved our little pond, and in hindsight we learned a great deal there and it probably cemented our lifetime's love for fishing.

We had mastered the art of casting and operating the fixed spool reels, and had become quite proficient at this. We had tried both crust and then dough, kneaded into a small ball in our fingers, and learned that the dough was a better bait. We discovered from trial and error that when things were slow, a gentle lifting of the rod would impart some movement to the bait and this would often lead to a take. The movement was important. And we had found that the first twitch of a float was not the one to respond to. You had to contain yourself for that heart stopping sliding away, or a good solid downward movement of the bubble, before you struck.

We also learned how to use a landing net and how to handle the fish carefully and gently with wet hands and fingers so as not to "burn" their skin. And to balance the little fish upright in our hands in the water as they recovered before darting back to rejoin their shoal to live for another day.

It was also important for us was that we caught something; made us want to go back. We kept a record of our results and the best catch I had in any one day was thirty five, and most days it would be about eight or nine of the handsome little fish. There was rarely a blank day. This sort of action is very important to sustain the interest of any youngster learning how to fish, and access to a pond or a stretch of canal where there are rudd or perch is ideal for this.

I can't recall exactly when or why we stopped fishing at Ballycorus, but I suppose it happened gradually as we grew up and moved on to other things. But it had done its job in whetting our appetites for fishing and we had thoroughly enjoyed it. Many years later I returned out of curiosity to see what had become of the pond. I parked my car and searched for quite a while but could find no trace of it. I double-checked my memory to make sure that I was in the right place and I'm sure that I was. Nothing remained of the pond, just a few bungalows standing where I was sure the entrance to it had been. It had vanished without a trace.

Glorious Saint Patrick

To an Irish trout fisherman there is something special about March 17th, the feast day of our Patron Saint and our national holiday. It is for most trout anglers the traditional first day of the fly fishing season, particularly on the river. Preparations would be in hand for days before to make sure that everything was in order for the river. Reels would be pulled out and checked over, with perhaps a little drop of sewing machine oil applied. Rod rings would be inspected and any loose bindings repaired. Fly boxes would be checked through and any missing or damaged favourites would have to be replaced.

As youngsters it was just like that for my fishing pals and me. I can remember how first Mass on the feast day morning always had a wonderful atmosphere of anticipation about it. At eight o'clock in the morning the church was always full of people who were determined to make full use of this special day. Anglers, bikers, mountaineers, walkers, horse riders, people heading for the famous RDS dog show, were all there together, sporting big sprigs of shamrock in lapel or hat and looking forward with great relish to enjoying a day out.

At the end of the service, as the final words of the wonderful hymn honouring Saint Patrick rang around the church, I always felt a great *relationship* with the saint. As though he belonged exclusively to us, and we to him. This day, when the rest of the world was all at school or at work, was a gift from him to us. It was very special and uniquely Irish and we were very conscious of our blessings on our big day, as we all joined in the great hymn,

On Erin's green valleys, On Erin's green valleys,
On Erin's green valleys look down in thy love.

Walking home from the church, past the gardens of nodding new daffodils and little coloured crocuses, the atmosphere seemed to be full of the Spring. There was always the sweet scent of rain and freshly mown grass, and everything seemed to be especially clean. And then, on this day when the fasting and abstinence of Lent were temporarily paroled, there was always a great breakfast to greet you as you came in from the church. Sizzling bacon, egg and sausages with black and white pudding from Hafner's wonderful pork shop in Henry Street, plates of hot buttered toast and marmalade, and cups of sweet tea to make sure that you were ready for whatever the day's weather might fling at you later on.

***

In my earlier years the fishing was usually incorporated into a family picnic, somewhere by a river in Wicklow. Beautiful places like Glenmalure or Glendalough, sparkling in the freshness of the spring.

Later, it meant a few pals pedalling happily off on our bikes to Loughlinstown or to the Dargle River near Bray, complete with flasks of tea and sandwiches and jam jars of worms that had been studiously kept in moss for the previous week to toughen them up.

Then on to fly-fishing with all the extravagant preparations. If the weather was mild with our traditional soft southwesterly breezes we were lucky. But Saint Patrick's day could bring you anything in the way of weather, from snow to frost to rain to towering gales, and even warm sunshine if you were really lucky! We took what came our way and got on with it. The only *real* disaster was an unexpected flood in the river, with water too high and too coloured for fly fishing. That meant a change of plan, meant rooting under stones for a few worms, but we always managed to fish and almost always went home with a trout or two between us.

As we got old enough to enjoy a pint, and the licensing laws were finally changed to allow the pubs to open on our national holiday, we would always head from the river to a nearby pub to ease the thirst of the day. Inside the cheery pub the atmosphere would be carnival, bubbling with talk about all the events of the day from the traditional Saint Patrick's day parades, to horse racing, hurling, fishing, or whatever else happened to be going on. The counter would be lined with pints of black stout, thick creamy heads in various stages of settlement, ready to drown the shamrock, and one after another, people would sing or play a tune on a fiddle or dance a jig or two, in one great convivial party. The *craic* was always mighty and as 'refugees' from suburbia we always fondly believed that life in the country was like this all the time and maybe some day, luck and work permitting, we too could live away from the city and enjoy all of this, all the time.

***

I often hear complaints that March 17th is too early in the year for a national holiday, that the weather is too cold, the daylight hours too few. For a fly fisherman, the timing is exactly right. Flies are starting to hatch again, trout are livening up after the cold of winter, and with the approach of Summer Time, or 'new time' as it is affectionately called, the whole of spring and summer beckon, with those wonderful long evenings to enjoy.

It's a fabulous day, for all the people, and there is just so much to enjoy.

Dunmore East

The entrance to Waterford Harbour, where the three sister rivers - the Nore, Barrow and Suir - finally embrace the Atlantic Ocean, is guarded to the east by the handsome lighthouse of Hook Head, with its striking black and white hoops, and three miles away to the west, by the picturesque little fishing village of Dunmore East.

In the 1950's and early '60's Dunmore was not the well-known holiday resort it is today. Fishing was much more important to the village economy than was tourism, and in fact it was much busier there in the winter when the herring fleet was in than it was in the summer, when it was relatively quiet and sleepy.

As kids we were unbelievably lucky to be taken every summer for a caravan holiday to Dunmore, and it was there that I first got hooked on sea fishing. There were no official camping sites or caravan parks in those far off days and the handful of holiday caravans used to park right down close to, almost in, the harbour. There was a great camaraderie among the families who regularly holidayed there, and all of us became very close friends, both children and adults alike. In most cases these were really strong friendships that often endured for lifetimes.

Dunmore was an absolute paradise for me. The seas around it teemed with an incredible variety and richness of marine life. During August, shoals of sprats (or *scraps*, as my kids later called them) used to appear close inshore and these were hunted up and down the coast by vast shoals of mackerel. And offshore, we were quite used to seeing schools of porpoises, small whales about the size of dolphins, rolling through the water with loud gasps of exhaled breath, as they in their turn chased and harried the mackerel shoals. We often went swimming in the darkness of night and, if the weather was warm and still, it was common to see flaring trails of phosphorescence around every swimmer as the masses of plankton were disturbed. During hot calm conditions, the basking sharks were a fantastic sight as they cruised along the surface through the plankton shoals, huge mouths gaping, dorsal fins as big as dinghy sails. There were many other less frequent visitors too; tope, dogfish and bass, and the strange little garfish with its swordfish-like bill, whose arrival usually meant we were in for a spell of very hot weather indeed. And the small but busy fleet of trawlers used to bring in wonderful catches of the very finest of fish of so many different species.

The first thing I used to do each year on reaching Dunmore was to rush up to the little post office in the centre of

Dunmore East, late 1950's
A trawler slips past the old sail-driven Pilot boat.
Mens Cove and the Old Red Sandstone cliffs in the background
- home to thousands of nesting kittiwakes.

the village and buy a mackerel spinner - the simple old red and silver type, which I think used to cost about six old pence - and a length of hand line wound on a wooden frame. This transaction was always a statement of intent of what I planned to do for the next three or four blissful weeks. Fishing from the rocks, I got to know every nook and cranny of the three miles or so of cliffs and coves going west towards the little cove of Portally: Black Knob, Flat Rocks, Red Head, Murray's Cove, Persecowan - I knew them all and the often dangerous and obscure ways to climb down the crumbly sandstone cliffs to reach the rocks and the sea below.

I can still remember the feeling of elation as I walked along the little path that wound along the top of the high red sandstone cliffs on a summers day, dressed in shorts and a sloppy joe singlet, and wearing just a pair of canvas shoes. Time meant nothing. I would sit among the flowering thrift, half asleep in the heat of the sun, watching for any signs of mackerel in the sea a few hundred feet below. I would look for any unusual patterns of dark and shade out in the shimmering sea, or for activity among the gulls. Usually they would be sitting on the water or on the rocks, almost comatose in the heat, heads turned back between their folded wings as though nothing in the world would disturb them.

Then, if I was lucky, which was often enough to seem like almost always, there would be little subtle signs of change. Perhaps somewhere along the sleepy rocky shore, the tumbling and clamouring of three or four gulls over a slightly darker patch of water. Other gulls noisily taking off, flapping awkwardly, and flying towards the scene to join in the confusion. Maybe some terns would appear, the graceful swallows of the sea, experts at diving for sprats and always a sure sign of fish. Excitement growing, until finally the water below the raucous mob of birds would seem to boil as the mackerel burst to the surface after the desperately fleeing sprats. Running to the nearest safe route down the cliffs, I would slide and slip on my backside down the red, sandy, grassy track to the rocks below and run and skip across the rocks to the scene of the action, hoping that the shoal would not move too far away from me. Looking into the clear water, thousands of silvery sprats swimming in an endless stream parallel to the shore, and often in a small inlet, a whole mass of them trapped by the insatiable horde of mackerel outside. Often I could see the mackerel, sleek shadowy forms with their green and blue stripes, moving incredibly fast into the shoal causing sheer mayhem, and watch as the water erupted in a spectacular burst of splashing as though a shower of giant hailstones had suddenly hit. Shaking with anticipation, coil the hand line on the rocks, foot on the wooden frame, and like David with his sling shot, twirl the weight and spinner around and hurl them out into the boiling mass. Pulling back fast, almost immediately there would be a sharp tug, and there would be the silver belly of a mackerel, turning and twisting in the clear sea below. Pull it in, shake it off the hook and out with the spinner again, quick before the shoal moves on.

Then, after who knows how long, trudging back up the cliff path with maybe twenty mackerel threaded through the gills on a length of string, and triumphantly home, hungry, thirsty and totally content. And fried mackerel fillets, straight out of the sea, sizzling on the pan for tea.

***

Later we graduated to rod and line using the German Sprat, a silver lure that could be cast a prodigious distance because of its weight and streamlined shape. I can remember fishing one evening at the Flat Rocks beside a hilarious character who had come out from Waterford on his old motorbike for the evening. He had a very powerful rod and was able to send his sprat out an awesome distance, way beyond

Dunmore East, 1949
Traditional mackerel fishing off rocks. All in their Sunday best, wellies notwithstanding!

our puny efforts. At one stage he obviously forgot to release the bale arm of the reel before hurling the lure seawards. There was a snap like a whiplash and I swear the thing was still gaining height as it disappeared out of our sight. 'Cripes, 'tis out to the Tower of Hook!' he said with a tinkle of laughter, watching his lure speeding towards the lighthouse three miles away on the Wexford coast.

The old traditional method of catching mackerel off the rocks reflected the unbelievable profusion of the shoals that used to appear in those days before the fishing fleets of the EU hoovered them all up. A twenty foot long pole of a rod was used, to the tip of which was tied a slightly longer length of line, no reel. Then a length of heavy nylon with a torpedo shaped lead weight about six feet up from a mackerel spinner, or a single hook baited with a three or four inch strip of silver skin off the tail of a previously caught fish. This was called a 'last'. It was so simple and effective. The fisherman would stand on the rocks, clear of the swell, and swing the spinner out into the sea to one side of him and simply drag it parallel to the shore for the length of the rod before lifting out, swinging back, and repeating. If the sprats were in, and the mackerel shoals in pursuit, you could count on a fish every time. Often the man would have a small boy (me, if I was lucky) as a helper to shake the mackerel off the hook when he lifted them in to the rocks, allowing him to carry on with minimum delay. It was a real honour to be given this job, a sign of trust, and made one feel very important indeed. Almost as good as fishing itself.

***

We were spoiled with the variety of fish that swam the seas around Dunmore in those days of plenty. There were congers to be caught in the harbour, and out at sea there were big golden pollack and coalfish, tope, wrasse and the very occasional bass.

Bass were very rare and usually were only caught by accident when trolling a rubber eel for pollack down at Middle Head, but there was one occasion when my pal Davy and I were in exactly the right place when a school of them came into the bay near Counsellor's Strand. We had rowed out to fish for mackerel when we saw some commotion among the gulls over near Counsellor's, an unusual spot for fish to be seen, so we headed that way to find out what was causing the excitement. As we neared the frantic gulls we could see lots of sand eels in the water but none of the usual signs of mackerel breaking the surface, so we picked up the rods and started to cast our spinners towards the activity. First cast we each felt a savage take and quickly we realised that these were not mackerel. They were heavier than mackerel and fought like demons, definitely not pollack either. To our amazement we had a bass each, both beauties of about three pounds.

For the next hour we had tremendous sport, catching about a dozen bass each, all in the three to four pound range. If we didn't actually hook a fish on every cast, we would see three or four shadowy shapes chasing the lures as they wobbled back in towards the boat. We had never seen so many bass before, and quite suddenly within an hour or so they were gone again and it was all over. In all the years that we spent at Dunmore that was the only time we saw or heard of a genuine school of bass appearing out of the blue like that.

***

One hot summer's day at almost dead low tide, six or seven very big grey mullet appeared in the harbour close to where the old Harbour Masters' house used to be. They were very impressive looking fish and a small group of us were watching them grazing and browsing in the sun just below the

Dunmore East, 1949
The bare essentials! A rod, a length of line and a mackerel spinner were all that you needed.

surface, close to where a big wooden lobster storage crate was moored half awash in the harbour. We were happy just watching these big fish, knowing them to be uncatchable. We had all tried before and we knew! They were too shy and much too smart.

Amid a cloud of red dust, Val arrived along in his old battered VW beetle and ambled over to see what the excitement was. He watched for a few minutes and then strolled purposefully over to his car, took out a rod, and started to tackle up with a very small float, a few pellets of split shot and a tiny hook.

He left the rod leaning against the rails of the steps and wandered off to the inner harbour where he found some small, red worms in the stalks of the seaweed exposed by the low tide, and he baited up with a couple of these. Then he called over a youngster who was idling about in a rowing boat and asked him to ferry him quietly over to the floating lobster storage crate which could easily take his weight without becoming completely awash. The big mullet had shyly moved away, but soon they were back again, nosing about very close to where Val's little red float bobbed on the water. We watched sympathetically from the pier.

The mullet passed by the float a few times, ignoring it completely, until at one stage Val gave the line a little tweak which must have caused the bait to move attractively in the water, because quite suddenly one of the biggest of the fish turned towards the bait and the float bobbled and then slid enticingly after him. Val struck and the big mullet sped away like an express train towards the mouth of the harbour. The impossible had been achieved!

With great encouragement from an ever growing rabble on the pier, Val skilfully played the mullet around the lobster crate, taking great chances with his light tackle whenever the big fish tried to run towards any of the rowing boats moored close by. We wondered how he would land the fish, even if he did play him out. Did Val want the young fellow in the boat to come and help him? Ferry him back into the steps, perhaps, where he might have a chance of beaching the fish? 'No thanks lads, I'm grand,' said Val, busily concentrating on the fish.

Eventually, after a mighty battle, the fish was obviously tiring and Val coaxed it in towards the crate, the top of which was submerged about four inches or so on the side where he was standing. He slid the mullet over the submerged edge of the crate and simultaneously stepped nimbly back a couple of paces to the opposite side, which slowly sank several inches under his weight while the other side rose correspondingly, leaving the eight or nine pound mullet flapping high and dry on the slats of timber.

It was a brilliant piece of thinking and fully deserved the cheers and claps which the chastened members on the pier generously rendered while Val carefully unhooked the mullet and returned it safely to the water.

Legendary stuff, discussed at length for years over large bottles of stout in Bill the butchers public house!

**

The most exciting Dunmore times for me were the idyllic days I spent out on the trawlers. In those days the trawlers went out at about five in the morning and returned at maybe eight in the evening of the same day. It was very rare for a boat to remain at sea overnight, although they would often stay in another small fishing port instead of returning to Dunmore. From the time I was about twelve or so the fishermen were delighted to take me out with them and one of them used to tap on the door of the caravan, or shake the canvas of our big tent, to wake me as they passed down to the harbour. I would hop out of bed, pull on my clothes and hightail it down and onto the

Dunmore East, 1951
Idyllic days on the trawlers
Author (standing on the ropes), brother Dick and fisherman friend Paddy "Matty" Power

boat to watch all the preparations. I loved listening to the big diesel engine starting up as two men cranked the starting handle and the coughing sound changed to a rich 'thuff thuff thuff'. Then all ropes away and I would sit right at the stern and watch the water swirling and churning behind the propeller as we pulled away from the quay in the early morning light. In shifts of two we would go below for breakfast of bacon and eggs and steaming mugs of tea. When I got a little older, and our course was a safe one heading straight out to sea, I would be left in charge of the wheel while the skipper and one of the crew had breakfast together. Then, handing the wheel back to the skipper, it was my turn to have the big fry-up down below with the second crewman.

The trawling itself was pure magic. At a spot selected by the skipper we would cut speed to slow ahead and out would go the marker buoy, followed by endless yards of rope, a huge length of nets, then more rope, the entire gear forming a big triangle as we ended the loop back at the first marker buoy. Then, having picked up the first buoy and taken a turn of rope around the winch, we would start to trawl for an hour or so, the little boat just keeping enough engine power to keep the net moving slowly forward along the unseen sandy bottom. This was always a very relaxing time of chat and song while nets were mended or other jobs attended to on the boat, and then came the excitement of winching back the net and revealing goodness knew what. Seaweed, crabs, and some fish could be caught in the leading part of the net and then finally the purse of the net, the bag itself, would come into sight and would be swung on board on a derrick and dangled over the deck for one of the men to pull the cord and release the catch. I would be standing well out of the way at this stage as the great mass of fish spilled out. The main catch were real quality bottom fish like plaice, sole, flounders and turbot but the catch would always include some surprises. Congers; john dories with the legendary thumbprint of Jesus Christ on their side; big snapping dogfish and tope; weird looking monkfish with huge grotesque heads and jaws; edible crabs and big gangly spider crabs. There was always something unusual to see. Then the nets would be prepared for another shot and, while this was being trawled, the men would be working hard again cleaning and sorting the previous catch before the next lot came on board. Then finally, maybe seven or eight o'clock in the evening, burned crisp by the sun and wind, we would head for home, trailing a screaming mob of excited gulls behind the boat as the last of the cleaning was done.

It was always a great feeling standing on the deck by the wheelhouse as the boat pulled in around the mouth of the harbour and the little crowd of curious spectators shuffled along the pier towards our mooring position. I felt like a fisherman, and the skipper would always find some job for me to do when we tied up, sweeping up or stacking boxes, making me feel useful and wanted and part of his crew. Somehow they always knew how important that was to a young boy. Then the boxes of sorted fish would be hauled with ropes by two men up the wall onto the pier and loaded onto a lorry to be taken off there and then to the Dublin market. I was always welcome to take whatever fish I wanted and I would bring home to my delighted mother the best of black sole or plaice, or maybe a couple of red gurnard or a johnnie dory as a special treat.

My best trawling friend was John Roche who owned and skippered a boat called the *Saint Joseph*. John was one of the most patient and persevering men I have ever met and I never saw him get angry about anything no matter what went wrong. He had a magic knack of always making you feel that he was delighted to have you along. The *Saint Joseph* was quite a small boat, varnished in light brown, and immaculately kept by John and his two crewmen. It had the classic lines of the small inshore trawler with a high, wide bow ahead of a large open deck area, and a neat little wheelhouse at the stern. I used to stand outside the wheelhouse chatting to John through the open window and listening to him singing as we ploughed through the waves leaving a lovely wake astern of us. In bad weather we would crowd together into the wheelhouse and I would watch the spray lashing across the glass and wonder to myself what it must be like in the freezing cold of winter when the herrings were running and any day missed might cost the boat dearly. It would be no place for the faint hearted.

One day I met John down at his boat and asked would it be OK to go out with him the following day. 'I'm going out tonight at eleven o'clock - would you like to come?' This was a very unusual time, and the wink of his eye told me it was slightly 'offside', making me doubly determined to go.

It was dark as we pulled out of the harbour, and instead of heading for the open waters to starboard, John pointed the boat up the estuary towards Waterford. We went about three or four miles, beyond Creadon Head, before the nets were shot, each dan buoy having a bicycle light tied to it so that we could find it again in the dark.

There was an electric atmosphere of expectation, flavoured with a definite hint of risk, as the buoys were picked up and we started to trawl. As we recovered the vast length of rope I could see John assessing what was happening out astern of us. I felt a wave of excitement as he told me that, from the engines labouring and the strain on the winches, either we had made a tremendous catch of fish or else we had picked up a mass of seaweed that was trapping sand in the net. We winched on, excitement growing, until suddenly the boat lurched forward and the trawl ropes went slack. It had indeed been a mass of weed and the huge weight of sand that it trapped was too much for the nets to take and they had ripped and torn, releasing the enormous weight. I felt awkward and helpless in what was obviously a moment of serious loss and disappointment. But John just smiled and shrugged, *'That's the way it goes'*, and as we headed back towards the harbour lights of Dunmore he sang like an opera star, as though he had just won a million dollars!

***

One year we got an unforgettable heat wave that lasted a fortnight or so and brought with it a crop of unusual visitors. For a few days before the real heat we had been catching the occasional garfish on our mackerel lures, strange little fish about two feet long, almost eel-like but with a four inch beak like a mini swordfish. Their appearance always heralded the onset of very fine weather and usually also the arrival of very big shoals of mackerel.

That heat wave was a cut above the average. For days the sun glared down out of a cloudless sky as each afternoon the temperatures soared into the nineties and Dunmore became a deserted village with people and animals seeking refuge from the stifling heat.

Late one afternoon a group of three of us headed out from the harbour in a rowing boat with a small outboard engine. The heat was incredible as we made towards the Hook lighthouse, searching the shimmering horizon for any unusual signs of activity. The combination of heat haze and flat calm made it quite difficult to distinguish scale or distance and it was hard to determine even how big an object was, or how far away. We could see two other small boats in the heat haze about half way to the Hook and we headed towards them to see what was attracting their interest.

We could see that there were a couple of people in each boat watching something in the water, and as we drew nearer we realised what it was. About a hundred yards beyond them we could see the nose, dorsal fin and tail of a huge basking shark and a little further away, a second one. We stopped the engine and sat back to watch, as always fascinated by the sheer size of these creatures. The bigger one must have been about twenty-five feet long and probably weighed about six tons. He was just cruising slowly along the surface through the plankton-rich water, huge mouth gaping in his almost oversized head, massive tail sweeping from side to side. Although these sharks are toothless and harmless, unless a small boat happened to get in among them and frighten them, they are nevertheless awesome because of their sheer size. Shielding our eyes and looking down into the sunlit water we could see, maybe ten or twelve feet down, a solid mass of small herring-like fish which we assumed to be pilchard. The dense shoal was almost stationery with a myriad flashes of silver as individuals turned momentarily on their back. A few hundred yards away, a small school of porpoises were obviously feeding on the pilchard and they added to the spectacular display, rolling and blowing together as a group in the calm sea.

Soon there were three of the sharks feeding quite close to us and it was quite eerie to just sit in the open rowing boat as every now and then one of them came within feet of us. As they approached, we could see into the huge mouths with their rows of gill rakers sieving the mass of plankton from the huge volume of water that passed through. Watching them, we got braver and braver until we actually started to row quietly after them and they seemed unafraid. We got so close behind one of them that I leaned out from the bow and touched his massive sweeping tail. It felt like heavy grade sandpaper and he just carried on slowly cruising forward, taking in gallons of water through his enormous mouth.

Then something extraordinary happened. One of the other boats started to manoeuvre towards the biggest shark and when it got to within about twenty yards of the monster one of the men on board picked up his rod and, for some extraordinary reason, cast his mackerel spinner across the back of the great fish. He wound in until the lure was obviously over the fish's back, and then pulled sideways to foul hook the shark. What happened next was scarcely believable. One would not expect such a huge creature to be so sensitive, but it obviously felt the small hook in its back, and with a sudden furious lashing of its tail, plunged away under the surface in a curtain of spray and broken water. For what seemed like many seconds we watched the bending rod of the startled angler until suddenly everything went slack, leaving the three boats in an eerie flat calm. In the heat-hazed silence, somebody unnecessarily asked, *'Lord save us, did you see that?'*

I can still recall clearly what happened next, perhaps because I just happened to be looking at the right spot. With absolutely no warning, the huge shark burst suddenly and shockingly six feet clear out of the flat calm water and fell back into the sea with a resounding crash, sending waves and spray and screaming gulls in all directions. It was awesome in its power and suddenness.

For ten minutes or so the three boats stayed there, occupants anxiously watching to see would the shark appear again. Every one of us just sat there, gripping hard onto the gunwales, silent and shocked and looking tentatively and apprehensively around at the sea that had become distinctly menacing in its stillness. *What if it resurfaced among the boats?* The thought of six tons of shark hurtling towards the surface directly underneath our flimsy open boat was a nightmare. The boat would be smashed to matchwood; we'd all be killed!

Although, gradually, something of an air of bravado returned to the three boats, I have a feeling that none of the spectators of that terrible leap will ever quite forget the stomach-churning fear as we waited helplessly for Armageddon. But the three sharks never reappeared.

***

67

During those brilliant 'Dunmore Years', opportunities came to fish many other waters beyond the much loved lakes and rivers of Wicklow. For Saint Patrick's days I used to stay with a great friend from Waterford, Davy McBride and his family, and fish the fabulous River Nore near Thomastown in County Kilkenny. This was a glorious trout river, and I saw for the first time really strong hatches of early season olives bringing on a terrific rise of trout. It paid to be at the river at about eleven in the morning, to catch a hatch that usually started about mid-day, and the sport was fast and furious in water that was perfect for wet fly fishing. Davy's mother, Nello looked after us like kings. We had fantastic packed lunches, the centrepiece of which was always a brilliant meat loaf which was Nello's own specialty. Even on days when Saint Patrick himself might have baulked at going outdoors, we had the strength to keep going until late in the afternoon when the river was quiet again and the light began to fade.

With Davy, too, I had some great fishing at Knockaderry reservoir outside Waterford and also on the lovely little trout stream at Jerpoint Abbey where idyllic summer's evenings were spent fishing the dry fly in the most splendid of settings right beside an ancient abbey, where the peace was such that you felt you were back in the twelfth century.

A Birthday Present

Although the cliffs and rocky coastline from Dunmore to Portally were a happy hunting ground for most of our fishing exploits, there was an awful lot more to be seen and done if we had access to a boat. A boat would allow us to reach many places and situations which were not accessible from the shore, and the opportunities for adventure became much more diverse. If we were really lucky and earned the trust of our adult mentors so that we were allowed to use an outboard engine, all the better.

When we were about thirteen, my pal Johnny and myself found a collection of battered lobster pots washed up on the rocks after a bad storm. This was treasure trove on a grand scale and, although most of the pots were very badly damaged, three of them were not too bad and we were able to secure the weights on the floor of the wicker frames and repair the torn netting so that they were almost as good as new. We managed to find an old cork float and a decent length of rope, also washed up on the rocks, and we were ready to try our hand at lobster fishing.

For bait we tried a multitude of things, from mackerel to old pollack to pieces of conger eel, and we set the pots outside the harbour along the rocky breakwater protecting the pier from the Atlantic storms, but with no success. Then we moved to the rocky headlands between the harbour and Lower Dunmore, but still caught nothing, not even an old crab or two.

One day we were chatting to two fishermen who were getting ready to put to sea to lift their own pots and they were asking us how we were getting on. No luck! They asked about bait, and how long we were leaving the pots before lifting them, and very diplomatically they suggested that our bait was not smelly enough and we were lifting the pots too soon. The very best bait for lobsters, they told us solemnly, was a "rotten rabbit", if you could stand the stench of it. But failing that, they said, you must use fish bait that has spent a good few days acquiring a thoroughly good smell of its own, preferably in a nice warm place in the sun! 'Try some of these,' they invited us, waving to a box filled with ancient fish that seemed to almost throb in the heat.

We baited up with the stinking fish and pulled our boat out to a concrete obelisk known as 'The Churn', which marked the navigable entrance to the harbour opposite the lighthouse, and set our three pots close in to it. Now that we knew we had the right bait we were full of renewed expectation and determined to be patient and wait at least twenty-four hours before lifting.

Next day we rowed out, picked up our little cork marker and began to pull the pots. The first one was empty, apart from a small crab, but as the second was pulled up towards the boat we could make out a brownish shape in the bottom that materialised into a fine edible crab and we were full of hope as we looked for the line that linked the second and third pots. To our consternation it was gone, we had lost one of our precious pots. Ah well! At least we had broken our duck with the crab, still had two pots, and had cracked the problem of the bait.

Three days later we went to 'borrow' some more evil-smelling bait from our two fishermen friends and told them about our triumph and our disaster. They were very sympathetic. How close to the Churn did we lose it? Were we sure of the exact place? We knew precisely where we had lost the pot because we had set it almost beside The Churn and the weather had been calm ever since, so it would not have been shifted by the waves. 'It's worth a try with a 'grapple'', the two men agreed, passing us up another half dozen ripe little flatfish for our two remaining pots.

We enquired around the harbour and finally found someone to lend us an old grapnel and a length of rope and set off at low tide to try the impossible. At best, we thought, we just might avoid losing the borrowed grapnel! When we reached the side of the Churn we agreed on what we thought was the exact location and though we peered into the water, about ten feet deep even at this low tide, the dark sea-weedy bottom made it impossible to see anything in detail. Johnny steadied the boat and I threw the grapnel out at the agreed spot. The iron quickly sank to the bottom and I began to pull it back, almost immediately feeling a resistance. Thinking that I had snagged a rock I pulled a little harder and lo and behold the weight came slowly towards me. Out of the dappled, trailing fronds of brown seaweed an unmistakable shape materialised. Our precious lobster pot, missing for three days, and snagged first shot with the grapnel! Johnny and I stood together in the stern of the boat and peered into the sunlit water, and as we slowly pulled so as not to dislodge it, something vaguely bluish could be seen through the mesh of the pot. Hardly believing our eyes, we gently pulled on and slowly the pot broke the surface and was grabbed by two eager pairs of hands and hauled, dripping, into the boat. We stared at the pot, and at each other. Not one, but three lobsters huddled in the bottom, and not a trace of the bait left on the securing cord. By a series of compensating errors we had hit the jackpot. Even in those days, before most of our shellfish found their way to the gourmet tables of France, a lobster was a rare luxury, a treat enjoyed by only a lucky few, and then only on very special occasions. And now here we were, with riches beyond our wildest expectations.

Two of the lobsters were smallish, though well above what we had learnt on the trawlers to be the minimum size.

The third was a fine specimen of about two pounds. We tossed a coin and Johnny got the two smaller ones and I the big one.

By sheer coincidence the following day was my mother's birthday. I can remember feeling a great sense of anticipation as I realised that, for a change, I had an opportunity to give her a really nice present. I swore Johnny to secrecy about the lobster and we hid it in an old disused fish house in a big bucket covered with lots of wet seaweed and with a plank of wood and a massive stone on top.

The following morning before anyone else had stirred I dressed and ran off to get the lobster. 'What has you up so early?' asked my mother, as I stood at the caravan door, wished her a Happy Birthday, and handed her the battered old bucket.

I watched her face light up as she carefully lifted the seaweed aside, and looking back, I think her expression of surprise and delight must have been a bit like mine when I found the little silver reel under all the coloured wrapping those few Christmases before.

Wilhelmina

Most of the families who holidayed in Dunmore in those days took their family pets with them, usually dogs of various shapes and sizes. We used to take our golden cocker, Grouse, and also a Siamese cat called Ambrose who travelled as well as any dog and was totally, at home in his temporary environment, amusing himself by terrifying all the dogs that wandered near our caravan. His favourite trick was to lie in wait on top of the harbour wall and jump down onto an intruding dog's back, sending the unfortunate animal on its way in a cacophony of wounded yelps. But the most spectacular pet that ever spent a summer holiday in Dunmore had to be Willy the raven.

Willy had been found as a small fledgling under a cliff in Wicklow and brought to Val, who was by now only a year away from becoming a qualified vet. Val had the most incredible way with all creatures and in his subsequent practice he would take on and heal the weirdest of animals with the most bizarre of complaints. The more unusual the patient, the more he loved to treat it. But he had a particular love and understanding of birds, and was a superb authority on them, even down to mimicking their calls with the utmost perfection. He was, of course, delighted to be given the opportunity to rear Willy and in a short time they were talking to each other in soft kronking sounds, Willy's head tilting sideways like a dog, her intelligent brown eyes following his every move.

Willy was actually a female raven, and when this became apparent her official name became Wilhelmina, but she remained Willy for short! As she grew, she and Val developed a most extraordinary relationship, almost like a man and dog type of bond, and they became inseparable pals. She was fully grown when she came on holidays to Dunmore, by which time she was a very formidable looking bird, particularly as she hopped in her curious sideways manner towards sockless, vulnerable feet, protected only by a worn old pair of canvas runners. She was about two feet long from tip of beak to end of tail, and her feathers were as black as coal. Her legs and her massive curved beak were also black, and her eyes were as dark and intelligent as any mammal's were. She used to perch on Val's arm and they would converse in soft murmurings, seeming almost to understand one another. And it was a common sight to see Val's old Volkswagen beetle passing through Dunmore village at a sedate twenty miles per hour, with Willy flying faithfully along outside, a few feet above the roof.

***

On this particular holiday Val and his family were staying in Lawler's hotel in Lower Dunmore, about one air mile from our caravan, which was still parked down at the harbour. Willy used often visit the harbour area alone and she would sidle up to a caravan to see what titbits might come her way, or to spread her huge wings to intimidate one of the dogs. She was the only living creature that Ambrose, the fearless Siamese, would not tackle. When Willy called, Ambrose disappeared. We were always delighted to see her, and she too enjoyed these visits and gradually came to know and to trust us. That summer became known in family folklore as 'Wilhelmina's Summer'.

Willy was a great timekeeper and if she was coming to visit it was always at about two o'clock in the afternoon. One day she arrived right on cue and hopped in her comical sideways fashion to the caravan where my mother was sitting in the sun shelling hard boiled eggs for a salad. Willy was very interested in this, her head cocking from side to side as she watched with her big brown eyes. The shelling continued for a while and eventually my mother held out a whole egg to Willy who sidled cautiously over and gently took the egg from her in her massive beak. She hopped a few feet away, placed one wicked looking claw on the egg, and began to pick small bites from it with her big hooked beak, obviously delighted with herself. She finished about half the egg and then took the other half and hopped purposefully over to the harbour wall which was about twenty yards away from the caravan. The ten foot high wall, made from Old Red Sandstone, was full of little holes and fissures between the massive blocks, and Willy found a nice sized hole big enough to take a mans fist and pushed the uneaten half egg into it as far as she could. Then, to my mothers' amazement, she covered up the hole with loose pebbles from the ground, surveyed her handiwork, and headed home for Lower Dunmore.

My mother was again at the caravan the following day when Willy came back. She landed close to the harbour wall and, without any hesitation, hopped straight to the exact spot in the wall where she had hidden the egg, picked out the loose stones and contentedly ate the other half.

***

When Willy returned home to suburban Blackrock after her summer holidays she developed a very anti-social habit that was to be her undoing. She would fly off early in the morning, after the milkman had done his rounds, and would systematically work her way up one side of Val's road and down the other, piercing the tops of the Jersey milk bottles with her huge beak and sucking out the cream. The rich Jersey milk bottles were easily recognised by their green foil cap and she would never bother with the ordinary milk that didn't have the same creamy top.

In the end the other residents, patient and understanding as they were, had had enough, and although Willy was widely loved and admired, Val was asked to do something about her. It was a desperate dilemma for him. Willy was then two years old, fully grown, and totally integrated into a human environment. If released back to the wild she might not survive. Val couldn't take that chance. So, after much soul searching, the heartbreaking decision was made and a home for Willy was found at Dublin Zoo, where she was safely established in a big aviary with lots of other birds, and still had the human contact she loved so much. For Val, the parting with his great pal was very difficult. It was probably hard for Willy too, but she did settle in well in her new home and appeared to be very happy there.

I went to see her some months after she moved, and I recognised her straight away. She looked content, and her plumage glowed with health, but I wondered did she know me too, as she looked at me with those big intelligent eyes. I couldn't bring myself to visiting her a second time.

***

There was one other famous incident in Dunmore involving another member of the crow family and, not Val this time, but his mother, Ella, who also was a great bird fan.

One afternoon a jackdaw landed on the ledge of an open bedroom window of Willie Lawler's hotel and picked up a glittering lady's engagement ring from the dressing table. He flew onto the gutter running along the roof of the hotel and stood there, ring in beak, mischievously eyeing the small crowd of people who had gathered below, including the ring's distraught owner. The sea lapped against the wall a few yards from the hotel, certain disaster if the cheeky bird took off in that direction.

Val's mother happened on the scene and immediately took control of the situation. 'Has anybody got a set of keys?' she matter-of-factly asked the astonished onlookers, and when handed some, she rattled them noisily at the jackdaw to catch his full attention, and then tossed them enticingly up in the air in front of him. The excited bird lurched at the tumbling keys and promptly dropped the engagement ring which was deftly caught by one of the crowd below and handed back to its grateful owner. The keys also fell harmlessly to the ground, and Ella continued on her way as if sorting out such near disasters were simply everyday occurrences.

Conger!

The pier at Dunmore East, 10 o'clock on a dark, warm, sultry August night. Two fifteen year olds sitting five yards apart in the soft arc of the harbour light, legs dangling over the edge of the pier, each holding a line of thick binder twine that snaked down into the murky darkness of the water. On the bollard behind the boys, two fresh but headless mackerel and a very sharp and bloody wooden-handled knife. Across the harbour, in the Old Red Sandstone cliffs, occasional muffled protests as something disturbed the thousands of sleeping kittiwakes whose forebears had nested there from time immemorial; and above them, the cheery lights of the little fishing village.

The concentration of the two was intense as they waited for the slightest odd movement at the baits. They chatted now and then about everything and anything, but basically their minds were down there with the mackerel heads, two feet off the bottom and in against the harbour wall. The tide was half way in and rising, and the congers would be moving back to their resting holes and crevices in the harbour wall after their feeding trip at low tide when their lairs were exposed. The big congers in particular had their own favourite homes and would return to these time after time, and woe betide any intruders. The harbour wall, made of blocks of pebbly Old Red Sandstone, was riddled with ideal conger holes, and because of this, and the plentiful supply of good food from the trawlers, the harbour was a favourite haunt of the big eels. As one of the boys watched, he saw in the dim light a small oil spot burst on the surface close to his line. The boys had always been told that this was a sure sign of a conger. He shifted his weight slightly and leaned forward, every sense probing down the line, through the water to the mackerel head twenty feet below. His pal could sense the increased tension, and silence enveloped the little circle of light.

Through his concentration the boy felt a very slight *tap, tap, tapping* on the line. The two lads had caught many congers and knew just how delicately they could take a bait. He could visualize the fresh mackerel head, the congers favourite treat, secured on the four inch swivelled shark hook. He tried to imagine a big conger, maybe six feet long, gently sucking the fresh bait and releasing again, the only perceptible sign to the boy above being a slight scraping of the stone weight against the harbour wall. The boys had often watched congers take a bait in daylight, at low water where you could see them, and they knew how patient and wary the big fish were. Try to interpret the slight tapping. Is it a conger? Or just another crab ruining his decent bait down there among the fishy skeletons that littered the harbour floor?

The tapping continued for about a minute and the boy tensely told his pal, 'There's something down there, could be a conger'. He shifted his balance again, kneeling on one knee on the pier as every sense strained for a give-away movement. The tapping ceased, and was replaced by a sense of the line becoming almost imperceptibly heavier. The boy's senses struggled to confirm that this was real. The apparent increase in weight was so gradual, so gentle, that it was difficult to distinguish the reality of it from a simple tiring of the arm. Could it be a conger, having taken the bait, slowly and smoothly backing away with it, so gently as he knew they could, nothing moving except for the almost metachronal action of the pectorals and huge dorsal fin? In five seconds he made up his mind. He was certain that the line was getting heavier, that something down there in the blackness had taken the bait. In one continuous movement he stood up and yanked hard on the coarse binder twine. Below him, in the darkness of the oily water, there was a fierce resistance, a twisting, jerking movement almost pulling the line from his fingers as he tried to balance on the edge of the pier. All sense of delicacy and caution were gone and the power he felt through the line was immense. His pal watched, looking from his struggling friend down to the oily water and back again.

First thought was to try to haul him up a few feet, don't let him back into his lair to wrap his powerful tail into the back of it. He had seen many big congers lost in this way, had heard the fishermen tell them many times, *'If he gets back in there, you might as well try to pull the pier down!'* As he heaved he could see, almost hear, the line hissing back and forth on the surface as the fish shook its head and snaked violently from side to side. Thank God for the swivelled hook. He knew that this was a big one, wondered could he handle it. As he took stock of the situation he began to panic, to realise that the fish was too big, too heavy for him to pull all the way up the wall, fifteen feet or more.

His pal, too, was reconnoitering the scene. Fifty yards to their left some steps ran down into the water, but the mooring ropes of a trawler tied up to the quayside prevented them walking the fish in that direction. There was no salvation in the other direction either, no other steps! They could either take a chance and try to pull the fish up the harbour wall, or haul it the shorter distance onto one of the trawlers.

Slowly the indistinct grey-white shape of a big conger loomed out of the dark water. They watched, almost in dread, as the massive eel twisted and shook its head in fearsome defiance until the boy finally wrestled it to the surface. It was decision time. The longer the fish was held, gyrating madly, the more likely it was that the line would kink and break or the hook would simply straighten out.

Immediately he tried to pull the fish clear of the water he knew it was too heavy for him to get it up to the top of the wall. Frantically they looked for someone to help, but they were alone. The twinkling lights of the village winked back at them, but the harbour was deserted.

The only chance was to pull the eel up the five or six feet onto the trawler right beside them. Quickly they agreed the plan and the second boy swarmed down the iron ladder and onto the deck of the boat. Fortunately they had been fishing inside the stern mooring ropes and had clear water to manoeuvre the conger towards the boat. The conger was feeling heavier all the time and showed no sign of tiring as it thrashed about below them. The second boy reached out and caught the line and held tight as his pal above let go and followed him down the rail to help. Together they manhandled the big eel out of the water and managed to get it up and over the gunwale onto the deck, hopping out of its furious path as it slithered over the side.

Keeping a respectful distance, they looked at the fish as it snapped and writhed from side to side on the deck. It was much bigger than anything they had ever caught before; there was no doubt about that. Must weigh about forty pounds. Its size and strength were awesome and the powerful jaws, with their needle sharp teeth, were like a bear trap. In the dim light, amid the smell of ropes and creosote and diesel, they got the big eel to bite on a wooden board and after subduing his body under a piece of old tarpaulin, they managed to grab him so that they could free the hook. Then carefully, with the aid of a shovel and the handle of a brush, they manipulated the snapping conger back over the gunwale and watched as it fell with a loud splash into the harbour, the reflected light shattering into a million fragments as the eel disappeared back into the depths.

***

It had been some experience! Their conger fishing was over for that night, and that year. They had satisfied an urge they had had for years, to sit together 'down the dock' on one night of their holiday and try for a conger. Next year, please God, they would again scrounge two lengths of binder twine, buy two swivelled shark hooks from Gertie Burke, catch a couple of fresh mackerel, and do the same again. And the sense of the unknown, of danger almost, the excitement as the *tap, tap, tapping* began, would grab them again.

As they gathered up their gear they couldn't help wondering, as they had often done before, just what other surprises lay hidden in the dark stillness of the quiet little harbour.

Mayfly

When I was about fifteen I paid my first visit to Lough Corrib, that legendary lake in the west of Ireland, where reality ends and the wonderland of Connemara begins. It was early June, mayfly time on the Corrib, and as I stood there on the shore of the lake on that first evening, it was clearly a very different world to the chattering, manageable streams and deep little mountainy lakes of County Wicklow. This lake was vast, even though there were islands everywhere, and looking out across the grey water I had a desperate feeling of being small. There was no sign of a rising trout as I looked at the vast expanse of lake and I wondered, not for the first time, how on earth I could reasonably expect a tiny fly to tempt a fish out of this vastness.

The following day was spent mainly mooching around the shore, clambering onto the big lime encrusted rocks and hopelessly casting a dry fly as far as I could into the marginal shallows of the lake. I watched the occasional boat drifting past the little islands and rocky promontories further out, wondering how they were getting on and hoping that my mother's promise of a few hours on the lake tomorrow would somehow work out.

My mother, in the meantime, was as usual not wasting her time! She had a pal called Petey Tierney, who sent her a beautiful Corrib trout by post every spring, and she had driven the couple of miles to see if he was fishing at the moment and if so, would he mind taking me out with him? As luck would have it, he was out on the lake when she called, so after a cup of tea and a chat, she left a message with his wife. That evening Petey himself arrived along on his bicycle and confirmed across another cup of tea that the fishing was good at the moment, that he was taking two anglers out in the morning, and yes, he would be delighted to have me along if I didn't mind doing a lot of watching!

***

I was dropped off on the shore at Petey's little harbour the following morning and introduced to the other two anglers. By eleven o'clock we were all ready, boat baled out, gear stowed and the three big dapping rods laid out along the seats.

The Corrib is not famous for its profuse hatches of mayfly and so the first task of the day was to capture a couple of dozen flies to dap with. Because of the scarcity of flies, this can be a frustrating and also an hilarious exercise, and I couldn't believe the sight of grown men (and me!) chasing a fluttering mayfly along the rocky shore with a landing net or a tweed hat. I learnt that they were best found in certain bushes. Mayfly seem to have a particular liking for the little stunted junipers commonly found along all the big limestone lakes and the most successful game plan was to position one or two 'catchers' armed with net or hat a few yards downwind of a bush, while the third operator gave it a good shaking. With luck, a fly or two would weave away out of the bush and the catchers would try to grab it out of the air or would set off in pursuit across the shore like some demented lepidopterists! Occasionally, too, it was possible to lift a freshly hatched fly off the water with a small minnowing net, but in all events it didn't matter what way you got them as long as you had enough for a few daps. The flies were kept in wooden boxes which had been designed and made by generations long gone, and each box would be unique and different from all others with its own arrangement of hinged doors, meshed air vents and hooks and rubber straps to keep things secure.

There were three rods fishing in our boat, one each in the bow and stern seats and Petey in the centre, also working the oar to keep the boat on its chosen drift. The dapping rods were massive things, sixteen or seventeen feet long, made of heavy greenheart with a bamboo top piece, and each reel had some backing and a length of floss blow line to which was tied a few feet of nylon and a special dapping hook whipped to the gut with yellow thread. This was baited with two, or in times of plenty, three mayflies which were allowed to blow out on the breeze ahead of the drifting boat and trip along the surface like a freshly hatched fly.

The Corrib is a wild place, as are many of the big limestone lakes in the west of Ireland, and legend has it that there are three hundred and sixty five islands on it, one for every day of the year. Some of these are just small rocky patches with a couple of stunted bushes growing on them, but others are true islands with lush pastures, grazing the most healthy looking cattle you ever saw. It is a perfect, natural wild trout fishery, almost entirely shallow water, with a profusion of food of all sorts. And in addition to its fine brown trout the lake also holds a great stock of pike, often of intimidating size.

Petey selected a drift to start the day and it wasn't long before we met the first of many trout. I was watching the dap of the angler in the bow, expertly kept sailing along the surface some five or six yards ahead of the boat, when out of nowhere and with explosive suddenness, there was a solid boil in the water and the flies were gone. It was so quick and so unexpected. I saw the man react immediately by lowering his rod and I felt like screaming at him 'your fly is gone, your fly is gone!', but of course he was well aware of this. For what seemed like an age, but was only in fact a couple of seconds, he waited and then he struck firmly upward and the long greenheart rod bent into a fine trout. The other two voiced their approval and kept fishing as the trout was coaxed around the bow behind the boat and played out safely there, well clear of Petey's oar. Finally, when the battle was over, Petey unshipped a net as big as a bicycle wheel and lifted the trout inboard with absolutely no fuss. He was in total control and seemed to be able to do any number of things, all at the same time.

I was as happy as could be just watching, when about half an hour later Petey hooked another fine trout and, with a big smile, said to me in his soft Galway accent, 'Take the rod'. I could see there was no denying him as he passed the rod to me and I took it from him with what must have been a grin like a Cheshire cat. The weight of the rod itself was something else, but the fact that there was a wild and very fit two pound Corrib trout on the far end of it made it even more difficult to manage. My heart was in my mouth as the fish threw himself out of the water a couple of times while Petey calmly told me to lower the rod each time, and then I had to try to persuade the fish around the stern, clear of the outboard engine, and play him out behind the boat. Once or twice I tried to manoeuvre the trout towards the boat too soon, and each time I was gently told not to horse him too much, just keep the rod up, let the rod play him. After a nerve-racking five minutes or so the net came out and was dipped in the water behind the boat and I felt that this was an approving signal. I started to lift the rod back to bring the trout towards the net and it was only then that I realised just how long those dapping rods are. I had reeled in too much line and I couldn't get the rod over my shoulder to bring the fish towards the boat without lifting him out of the water. So I had to release some line, very carefully so as not to give the trout any slack, and try again. Second time lucky, my three companions were delighted with me, and Petey insisted that I keep the rod and fish out the drift. It was brilliant. The instructions were few but important. Keep the fly, and none of the cast, on the surface, but don't let it drag. If you rise a fish, lower the rod to let him take the fly down, count to three and then strike. Sounds easy, doesn't it? But if you have been watching your dap for twenty minutes or so as if your very life depended on it and suddenly, without any warning whatsoever, it disappears in a flash of golden brown flank into a vortex of swirling water, it's pretty hard not to react. I was much too quick with the first fish I rose and never even touched him. But, well coached as I was, I gave the next one a little more time and when I struck there was a wonderful solid resistance and I was in one.

**

Thanks to Petey and the other two anglers I had a field day. They allowed me to fish every second drift and explained what to do and what not to do in such a friendly way. They explained what water they were trying to cover with each drift, and why, and the importance of rocky points and headlands as feeding stations for big fish, and the day just seemed to fly by.

When we finally pulled the boat ashore and made everything safe, I shook hands with each of them and made to say goodbye, and thanks. It must have been so obvious that I had really enjoyed myself. 'We'll have another day next year, please God', Petey smiled, holding out a paper parcel to me. In it were two fine trout wrapped in wet grass and it was hopeless protesting that I just couldn't take them.

My feet scarcely touched the ground as I sped back to tell all to the others. The day had been brilliant and I knew without any shadow of doubt that the mayfly and I were destined to become regular companions.

Mick and the Murchú

I sat in the sunshine on the lake side of the viaduct crossing the south Vartry Reservoir near the village of Roundwood in County Wicklow. From over the low wall behind me I could hear an occasional car murmuring by on the road but, by and large, it was quiet and peaceful and I was half asleep in the heat of the summer's afternoon. My feet were almost in the water as I idly studied a shoal of minnows directly below me. The wall of the viaduct sloped gently at about 40 degrees into the water and the minnows were enjoying the sunny shallows of the slope. But right beside them was one of several arches running under the roadway and connecting the main reservoir with a smaller overflow to the north, and here the water was dark and deep.

Suddenly, from the deeper water below the arch, a speckled raider dashed headlong into the middle of the shoal and, just as swiftly, turned and disappeared back from where he had come, presumably with one unlucky minnow. I had a perfect view of the attacking trout and the frantically scattering shoal of minnows.

What surprised me most about the incident was the sheer speed of the attack. One moment, just a shoal of contented minnows, next, in a split second of smash and grab, one gone. Swift, aggressive and highly efficient, striking like a bolt from out of the depths where he had obviously been watching his prey and waiting for his chance. I had always regarded trout as very serene creatures, feeding discerningly on carefully selected nymphs and adult flies which were carried past them by the current in the river, and scornfully ignoring anything which was not entirely to their liking. The fishy equivalent of cocking the little finger up as one sips the china cup of tea! What I had seen in the reservoir was a very different side of the trout's character, the predatory side of it, and there was nothing serene or gentle about it at all.

***

We were very familiar with the north and south reservoirs at Roundwood, but since a day permit was required to fish them, we generally tended to stick to fishing the Wicklow rivers, or Lough Dan, where the fishing was free. Sometimes we did spend our precious pocket money on a permit but on other occasions, as is the way of impecunious youth, we just took a chance and went ahead and fished. And needless to say, the element of the forbidden always added significantly to the excitement of the fishing. There is nothing more certain to get the adrenalin flowing than to trespass on forbidden waters! In any event, we always fished fairly with rod and line, and since we never did any harm or damage, we trusted that our venial sins were soon forgiven.

The south reservoir at Roundwood is particularly beautiful with a wooded shoreline all around, and there was in those days a very good stock of trout in it. Fish of a pound to a pound and a half were not uncommon. In March and April the water level was always very high after the winter's rain, in places right up to the path which ran around the three mile long lake, and fly fishing was extremely difficult because of the trees and bushes which grew right to the water's edge, sometimes even into it. But in July and August, when rainfall was low and water consumption high among the reservoir's customers, the level retreated dramatically and a shallow, sloping shoreline of twenty or so yards emerged so that you could wade out well clear of the bushes and cast a fly quite easily. At this time of year we saw plenty of rising trout, particularly in the evenings, but although we tried both wet and dry flies, we never seemed to stir more than the odd fish.

***

One summer's evening in late July as Ruaidhrí and I were dismantling our rods on the roadside, one of our local pals, a hilariously mischievous character called Mick, happened along on his way into the nearby village. We were explaining how we had contrived yet again to catch nothing when Mick casually asked, with a serious cocking of his head, had we ever heard tell of the 'Murchú'? It was a big brown fly, he explained, measuring off an inch with his thumb and forefinger, and it hatched out on summer's evenings on the reservoir, and the trout went mad for them. After hatching, it ran in along the water, he said, gesturing realistically along the saddle of his bike with two Woodbine-stained fingers, and it was then that the trout would take them, often with a ferocious rise. This was a bad evening to see them, he said, too much wind, you'd want a quieter sort of a night to see them properly. 'Keep an eye out for them now the next time you're here, and don't be packing up so soon either, it's much too early', he scolded us as he cycled off towards Sean's pub in the village for his pint of Guinness.

On the way home Ruaidhrí and I wondered about the Murchú. We had never heard tell of any such fly, and Mick was such a leg-puller that we couldn't quite believe it. But on the other hand, Mick had seemed to be dead serious, and his description of the hatching insects, and the trout's response, was fairly riveting.

A few days later I was in a tackle shop in Dublin getting a few flies for the river when, in a tray of sedge flies, I spotted a compartment labelled 'Murragh'. In the compartment there were several big, brown sedges with very prominent antennae, like nothing I had ever seen before. For a moment nothing clicked and my eyes moved on to the smaller river sedges, but then the penny dropped! 'The Murragh'. I picked one up and studied it in my hand. The body was about an inch long. Could this be Mick's Murchú? He must have know it by its Irish name. I had never seen such a big fly and I thought that it looked too cumbersome and bushy to fool any discerning trout. But I was gripped by the excitement of the discovery and I just had to buy a few, and the following weekend Ruaidhrí and I headed off to Roundwood to try them out.

***

It was a nice, warm summer's evening, with just a little cloud and a gentle breeze, and we elected to fish the shore with the breeze coming from one side rather than fish with the wind at our backs. We each put up a murragh and started to fish, casting the big dry fly out and leaving it sitting very conspicuously on the calmish water and looking most unlikely to accomplish anything other than to amuse any passing trout. We could see the odd fairly typical quiet rise well out from the shore but our murraghs remained totally ignored.

As dusk fell and the far shore faded into an indistinct blur, we were startled by a very aggressive rise some fifty yards out from us, very different to the previous quiet takes. A few minutes later, looking left along the shore so that we could see more clearly against the reflection of the evening sky, we noticed something scuttling erratically along the surface towards the shore. As we watched, there was an explosive rise under it and it disappeared in a big disturbance leaving two very interested anglers gaping after it. We saw another little trail on the water and realised that it was a large insect literally running along the surface of the water towards the shore. Wading over to intercept it, we saw that it was a big brown-winged sedge, with a brown body and prominent antennae. Mick's Murchú, alias the murragh, was also known as the

Great Red Sedge, as we read afterwards in Dick Harris's classic book "An Anglers Entomology".

We started to fish again, now very focussed all of a sudden, as trout began to feed closer in to us and the odd murragh came skittering in along the surface in the fading light. A trout rose about a dozen feet left of my fly and almost instinctively I began to twitch the fly in slow jerks back towards the shore. Within a couple of twitches it disappeared in a terrific boil and I tightened into a very nice fish. With a little bit of movement, the big brown blob of fur and feathers had suddenly become a very acceptable imitation of the real thing.

The rest of that evening was just brilliant. We rose eight or nine trout each, hooking just a few and I think landing a couple each. But it was the excitement and anticipation of the big hit as we twitched the murraghs towards us that was so special. In the tranquillity of the reservoir, the smashing, violent rises came so unexpectedly and I found myself thinking back to the trout I had seen at the viaduct, and the speed and determination of his attack on the shoal of minnows. This was the same side of the trout's character, determined that the fleeing sedge would not escape. We fished on into darkness, casting out, twitching back and waiting for the splash and grab, until all was quiet and the lake went to sleep for another day.

***

For the next few years we had great fun fishing the murragh on summer nights at the reservoir. By this time we were either working or at college, and we realised that the days of innocence were over, that we were beyond pleading that we couldn't afford a day ticket. So we always called to the engineer and bought one before we started to fish.

Appropriate justice for my few harmless indiscretions in not coughing up for a permit was done one evening when I was to meet my brother-in-law at the reservoir for a night's sedge fishing. It was a hot, sultry August evening with thunder in the air and I had been given a lift to Roundwood and walked the mile or so to where Bernard's car was parked in a grassy lane near our favourite part of the lake. His plan had been to arrive a couple of hours before me, buy a ticket for himself, and carry on down to the lake where I was to meet him at a pre-arranged spot later in the evening. 'If I'm not there by nine o'clock,' I had said on the phone earlier, 'It means I won't be coming at all.'

I changed into my waders, pushed my shoes well in under Bernard's car in case of rain, and ambled happily across a couple of fields towards the lake, full of the customary anticipation of an exciting evening despite the threatening looking sky. The engineer's house where permits could be bought was at least a mile further around the lake. It would take me a good hour to walk there and back, so after at least two second's deliberation I shrugged my shoulders and elected to fish away without a ticket on this occasion.

I tackled up when I reached the water's edge and began to fish. I knew that Bernard would be some distance further to my left along the shore and I intended working my way towards him, enjoying the fishing as I went.

With every cast I kept a look out in case someone should come and nobble me without my ticket, and sure enough after an hour or so, a boat appeared around a point further up the lake near to where Bernard was to have been. Feeling guilty, I reeled in and stepped back across the little path and out of sight among the Scots pines to wait for it to pass. I waited for ten minutes or so, wondering why the boat hadn't carried on down the lake towards me. I began to worry that the occupants, almost certainly members of the local angling club, must have seen me and had pulled ashore to come up the path behind me to check if I had a permit. The adrenalin began to flow as I crept like a fugitive through the trees away from the boat to escape the dreaded humiliation.

Silently and furtively I headed off down the shore in the opposite direction from the meeting point with Bernard. To compound my misery the sky gradually darkened and, amid loud clatters of thunder, big spots of rain started to fall. I must have gone about half a mile down the lake when the heavens really opened with what could only be described as a cloudburst. Cursing quietly but fluently to myself I looked at my watch. Nine o'clock had long since passed and now I was worried that Bernard might think I had not come at all. In this weather he might pack up early and drive straight back to Dublin. The safest thing to do was head back for his car and wait for him there, so I dismantled the rod and trudged back across the fields through the gathering gloom and driving rain to where the car had been parked. To my horror the grassy laneway was empty, except for my two soggy shoes, now half full of rainwater and looking utterly forlorn between the muddy tracks left by Bernard's departing car. He must have thought I wasn't coming and my lift home to Dublin was gone.

Muttering darkly to myself, I pushed the saturated shoes into my fishing bag and set off in my waders to walk the mile to the village where I hoped I might find someone driving back towards Dublin. By the time I got to Roundwood I was drenched to the skin and my mood was as black as the night. I pushed open the door of Sean Kavanagh's pub and squelched into the cheerful noisy atmosphere, and there was Bernard, dry as a bone, drinking a pint and enjoying a game of darts with the lads. A dozen faces grinned happily at my sodden figure, dripping in the doorway. And a familiar Wicklow voice broke the silence: 'Would you be able for a pint, Peter?' And the laughter began, led I have to say, by my own. It was Mick of course, puffing on his perennial Woodbine, his 'Biner' as he called it himself, and I have never seen his blue eyes twinkle with such mischief as he innocently asked me how the Murchú had done tonight?

Return to the Corrib

By the time I finished secondary school and started working we had become quite familiar with some of the lovely lakes and rivers of the midlands, only an hour or so by car from Dublin. We fished wet flies for trout on Lough Sheelin in the earlier part of the year, and had terrific fun on Lough Ramor fishing for pike. But I still had a yearning to revisit the Corrib, and so in early June of that first year of work I took a few day's holiday, hired a VW Beetle, and set off to cross the Shannon to the west again.

I headed again for Oughterard, that most picturesque of villages that at Mayfly time becomes a trout angler's paradise with an atmosphere that simply is *fishing*. I really had no plan as to how I was going to organise myself with a day or two in a boat. I knew that I couldn't afford to hire one on my own, my junior bank clerk's resources had all gone on the Beetle.

Lough Corrib, 1962
John Joyce (far right), author (second from left) and two Galway anglers after a day on the lake.

95

My best chance was to find a fellow angler who might be happy to share with me.

Although the hotel bar was relatively quiet early on that first evening, there were three men in one corner having a drink who were quite obviously fishermen. They were enjoying a typical animated fisherman's conversation as I came in and we smiled a greeting as I passed. After a short time I got chatting to the barman about the fishing and whether he might know of anyone who would be going out the following day or two who might like some company. Quite suddenly one of the three men stood up and came over to me with a friendly hello, and said that he hoped I didn't mind, they couldn't help overhearing that I was interested in a day on the lake. Pointing back at the table, he said that his friend John was going fishing one way or the other, and would be delighted to take me out. He told me that John was a ghillie with his own boat and the three of them had been fishing for the past few days. Since the dapping was just about over and John was going out anyway, he would love some company. 'Come on over and meet him and have a pint with us'. Delighted, I joined them for a moment, and since he and his friend were heading back to Galway, they left John and myself to have another drink and make a plan for me to meet him at his cottage at ten o'clock next morning.

It's funny sometimes how fate intervenes because that was the start of a great friendship. John was in all senses a remarkable man. In his fifties then, he lived alone with his grown up son, Barney, as his wife had passed away some years before. He was a resourceful man who had built his own cottage and his own boat, and he lived for the fishing. He was a great character, very much loved around Oughterard, an expert angler for both trout and pike, and he knew his beloved Corrib like the back of his own hand.

**

And some went fishing
The author, Val Demery, Michael Herriott, David Greaves, George Herriott

Photo 1

A classic Shannon trout
William McGrath admires Bernard Chadwick's 7lb 7oz brown trout taken on
spent gnat, Lough Derg, 1992

Photo 2

Dromineer Castle

Photo 3

Yellow Island, when the gnats go out

Photo 4

Lough Derg Sunsets

Watching for a rise
"for peace comes dropping slow"

Photo 5

Fancy a cuppa?
Michael & Al Herriott take a break. "Uncle Al" enjoyed his fishing until he
was ninety-two, weather not an issue

Photo 6

Photo 7

Haut cuisine, Lough Derg Style
Michael cooks the steaks!

Photo 8

Photo 9

Photo 10

Corrib Moods

A hopeless flat calm becomes a nice fishing wave in the time it takes to change a fly

The author with a fine 7lb 14oz brown trout taken on dry spent gnat,
Lough Derg 1994

Photo 11

A fish before lunch
Michael Herriott with a nice three pounder taken on dry brown sedge.
No wind for dapping, but the rods are ready along the seats

Photo 12

Magnificent Wilderness
A few stunted trees grow through the needle-sharp
limestone at Aughinish Bay, Lough Mask.

Photo 13

Ruaidhrí de Barra with a lovely four pound brown trout caught on
Black & Peacock spider, Lough Mask.

Photo 14

The following two days were pure magic. As we walked across the wet fields in the warm June sunshine to where John's boat was kept, we chatted about fishing, the lake and the mayfly, and the air was full of the wonderful coconutty smell of gorse and the heavy sweetness of the hawthorn. In the little nook where John's boat was pulled ashore, the water was calm and clear and teeming with little swimming creatures. Outside, the lake sparkled in the morning sunshine, with a nice wave on it prompting John to remark, as he baled the boat, that it looked like a fine dapping day. There was a promise of trout in the air and my spirits were soaring with the skylarks.

We fished for two days and I learned a great deal from John. He showed me where to find mayflies, either along the shore, in the long grass or in the gorse or juniper bushes, and how to put them on the dapping hook. He explained how to select a drift, the importance of natural features as feeding stations for the bigger fish. How to manage the boat on the drift and the value of keeping the two dapping rods well spread to cover the maximum water. And of course what to do when you met a fish! He knew Petey Tierney well and approved of the excellent tuition I had had so far, particularly when I managed to hook the first trout I rose.

Each day John brought with him a sod of turf soaked in paraffin and wrapped in an old newspaper, and when we pulled ashore for the grub he would use this to start a fire of dry sticks to boil his old black kettle filled with Corrib water. While the kettle was boiling he would invariably drink a bottle of stout by the neck and keep an eye on the fire. Then we would settle down for an hour or so and have our lunch of sandwiches and hard-boiled eggs and big slabs of rich fruit cake, all washed down with mugs of dark strong tea. And he would tell stories about the lake and the islands and headlands, and the great fish that had been caught at each landmark - and the ones that got away - until I couldn't restrain myself from packing things back into bags to hurry him out there again.

In the evenings, after stowing everything safely away in the boat and bringing just the fishing bags and petrol can, we would saunter back across the fields to his house and have a big meal of cold mutton and potatoes and wonderful cabbage, from his own garden of course. Then we would head off into the village for a can of petrol and a couple of pints of stout in Jim Egan's lounge where we caught up with all the fishing news of the day from up and down the lake and swapped yarns with whoever was there in the pub.

We caught quite a few trout in those two days and John insisted that I take most of them back to Dublin with me. 'Sure what do I want with them?' he asked, chewing on the end of his pipe, and there was no doubting that he meant it. I began to worry about how he would feel when I tried to pay him something for the two great days we had had. We had got on so well together and I didn't want to damage that in any way. On the way back to his cottage on the second evening I picked what I thought was a good moment and said, 'John, I'd like to give you something for the two day's fishing'. He turned to me with a toothy grin. 'Didn't we have the finest couple of days you could wish for', he said, and shaking his head, 'I enjoyed it anyway'. He spat with great finality into the grass and as we walked on across the field it was quite clear that the subject was closed.

Next morning on my way back to Dublin I called to his cottage to say goodbye and we chatted for a while at the door of the cottage, drinking the inevitable tea. He told me that for a month or so after the mayfly ends, the fishing would be very bad, the trout would be feeding on perch fry and would look at nothing else. But in July and August there would be great fishing again, dapping the daddy long legs and grasshopper; big trout would be caught, better than on the mayfly. He looked at me and rattled his pipe off the heel of his boot. 'Would you like to come down then for a few days?' he asked.

'Come and stay here with myself and Barney, 'tis handier altogether for the boat'.

As I turned the hired Beetle and waved to him before starting up the bohereen towards the Galway road I was smiling to myself at the prospect of it all, and July couldn't come soon enough.

***

In July I rode down on my new motor scooter, bristling with rods, nets, bags and all the usual paraphernalia. John was very impressed with the bike but there was no way that he could be persuaded up onto the pillion seat.

The collecting of the flies for the harry dapping was quite different from mayfly gathering, and even more hilarious! Daddies were best caught early in the morning when they were still a bit dozy. The best method was to walk through the long grass in a sheltered place until you disturbed one and then you simply caught it in cap or hand as it rose. The grasshoppers were another story and required a much more scientific approach! You had to wait until you heard one rasping in the grass and then walk slowly towards the noise. Invariably, the grasshopper would sense you coming and stop the rasping noise, but you just continued on towards the spot, sweeping your foot over and back in front of you as though you were probing for a landmine. You were best advised to stand upright while doing this, rather than to walk along with your face close to the grass, because that way you had a much better chance of following the first big leap of the grasshopper as he sensed something approaching. If you could spot where he landed after that first jump you had a fair chance of catching him, because the second leap was much shorter. If you didn't see where he landed after the first jump, start again.

The dapping technique was exactly the same as for the mayfly and the reaction to a take was the same. Drop the rod, count to three and strike nice and firmly but not too hard. We had a couple of marvellous days but I can remember in particular one classic moment when we were fishing in bright sunshine and fairly light wind through a perfect shallows no more than a couple of feet deep. The bottom was a golden calcareous sand studded with big round boulders of limestone, all beautifully dappled with light and shade and rippling shadows in the hot July sunshine. As I watched my dap like a hawk I saw a good trout materialise almost ghostlike from behind a big boulder and I held my breath as he tilted and rose quite purposefully towards the fly. Trembling with anticipation, I watched him swim slowly in a circle about six inches below the fly, inspecting every detail of it. *Go on*, I urged silently, *take it, take it!* But after a moment he seemed to lose interest and drifted away to one side. I was about to lift the dap to let the wind take it further from the boat when John quietly said, 'Leave it to him, Pether'. I didn't think he had even *seen* the incident. I managed to control my trembling hands and kept the dap sitting nicely on the water and quite suddenly there he was again, from nowhere, like a grey-brown shadow. Up he came, very deliberately, as though he had had a good think about it, and down went the grasshopper in a nice positive take. I lowered the rod, gave him a couple of counts, and bent the big dapping rod into a very handsome three pounder, speckled and spotted and golden as only a trout from the Corrib shallows can be.

***

That particular day hadn't finished with us yet. We ended up about three miles along the lake from John's harbour and gradually the wind had dropped and dapping had become impossible. At about five o'clock we decided to head back home as the wind was clearly gone for the day and John suggested putting out a troll. He selected a small Mepps from an old metal cigarette box and as he started up the engine I rigged this up with a couple of swivels and a small lead weight, and we settled down to enjoy the run home on a simply beautiful July afternoon. About twenty minutes later we were passing along by a small island when the rod gave a tremendous kick but fortunately stayed jammed behind the rowing pin and didn't jump out of the boat. Before I fully realised what was happening, John had turned the boat ninety degrees, knocked off the engine, and was urging me to grab the rod. When I did, I had to quickly loose the clutch or we would have broken in him straight away. There was a big fish out there and he was making some wild runs, bending the fibre glass rod and tearing tens of yards off the reel each time. My instincts were to stand up in the boat as I tried to pump line back but John, sucking away on his pipe, told me firmly to sit down. We battled on for half an hour at least, John quietly keeping an eye on everything; the fish, me, the boat, the rocks and shallows around us, and the big net he had. He told me afterwards that he had been sure that it was a very big trout. It never showed itself for such a long time, keeping well down and not performing the typical head-shaking leaps that a big pike will. But eventually we got him close and we could see that it was a pike. I could sense some disappointment in John. For him, a really big trout would have meant a lot; to his reputation and in the *craic* of his relationships with his fishing colleagues up and down the Corrib. A big trout would be talked about for years. He had of course many good trout to his credit but he knew this fish was in the twenty-pound bracket and would have dearly loved it to have been a trout.

His disappointment when he saw that it was in fact a pike was utterly transient. He could see how excited I was as we manoeuvred the tiring fish towards the boat and as it came alongside it was quickly and expertly gaffed. We weighed it on a spring balance back at the cottage and it was eighteen and a half pounds, for me a great pike, and I was absolutely delighted.

***

It was a dream end to a great fishing day. Half a dozen fine trout, including the ultra-cautious fish from behind the rock, and the biggest pike I had ever seen caught anywhere. I was very happy as I scooted into Oughterard that evening to fill the petrol can and get a few bottles of stout to bring back to the cottage to celebrate. I had one pint in the bar while I recounted our adventures to the other anglers and then headed back to John's place. As I neared the cottage I could see a small white van parked outside and as I pulled the bike up on its stand I could hear music coming out over the half door on the warm night air. Walking through the door of the cottage was like walking straight into a *céilidh*. There were about fifteen people there, young and old, boys and girls, men and women, most of them playing musical instruments, either fiddles or accordions or bodhrans, and there, in the middle of the stone floor, was the pike! By coincidence, a crowd of John's friends and relations from the other side of the lake had decided to pay him a visit and they came with bottles of stout and poitín and with all the instruments of a small band, ready to have a right good party. In due course everybody had to perform a solo act in turn and as the night wore on the *craic* and the music got better and better. It was spontaneous joy and it was all over too quickly at about 2 a.m. when they all had to go home. As they were leaving John took me to one side and hesitantly asked, 'would you mind very much if they took your pike? They wouldn't thank you for a trout, but the pike is a great treat for them'.

I can still see them all piling happily into the little white van, musical instruments, pike and all, and heading off up the bohereen. You can never plan an evening like that - they just happen, and you're lucky to be there!

***

I fished with John for a few more years, a day or two here and there, from the cold winds of March when a drop of poitín was required to restore circulation after we came ashore, to the heat of August days. On one or two days he had things that he just had to do, like organising his turf for the winter, and he would apologise and say how he just couldn't make it, but I should take his boat and fish away myself. His boat and his engine were his life and I realised how much he trusted me and I was very honoured by that. He had seen early on that I was reasonably competent in a boat, thanks to my days in Dunmore. But the Corrib, like many another Irish limestone lake, with its rocks, shallows and islands, requires the utmost respect, or an engine or boat can be damaged, or maybe even worse. I was careful and I stayed strictly within the area I had fished with John, and I actually managed to catch a few fish on my own.

***

When I left my job to return to full time education a few years later I lost touch with the Corrib. Although I did write to John once or twice a year, and always at Christmas, I only saw him once more. That was a few years later when I was working on a summer exploration job in Gort, Co. Galway, and my fiancée, Gillian, came down for a weekend. We drove the fifty miles out to Oughterard on the Saturday evening and down to John's cottage, on the chance that he just might be there. He was delighted to see us and after a long chat over a cup of strong tea the suggestion was made that we might go in to Master Jim Egan's hotel for a drink. John only rarely went into Oughterard at this stage and Jim greeted him like a long lost friend. 'It's all too seldom that we have the pleasure of a visit from John Joyce' Jim announced happily to the entire bar, 'and to celebrate the occasion I'd like you all to have a drink on me'. His delight at seeing John was a joy to behold.

When we were leaving the hotel John took me aside very tentatively and asked would we mind waiting for a minute, he would follow us out to the car. When he joined us we went back to his cottage and he made a pot of tea. We drank that, and reminisced about the days on the lake and the characters we had met and the fish we had caught and missed. It must have been three o'clock in the morning when we left and as we went to the car to drive home he pushed a paper bag onto the back seat and whispered to me, 'That's for the journey back to Gort'. In the bag were a bottle of stout and a 7-Up, which were what he had gone for while we were waiting for him outside Jim Egan's, and he had also included a bottle opener for good measure! John never travelled far from home, the odd ten miles to Maam Cross or an occasional trip into Galway being about as far as he would normally go, and in his estimation the fifty mile trip back to Gort was definitely a journey which would require a break for refreshments. It was so typical of him and our protests were not even heard.

At his cottage gate, in the wonderful silence and soft luminescence of a Connemara summer's night, we shook hands and said our goodbyes with an extraordinary feeling of affection for him.

Lough Ramor's Pike

Lough Ramor in County Cavan is a fine lake, about five miles long and up to two across. It differs from many of the other lakes of the Irish midlands in that it is not a limestone lake but is located on older, more acidic bedrock that gives the water a dark and inscrutable appearance. It is shaped like a boomerang, with the lovely town of Virginia at the elbow on the northern side of the lake. The River Blackwater, an excellent trout fishery, flows out of the eastern end of the lake and ambles through the rich meadows of Counties Cavan and Meath to join the Boyne at Navan.

On Sunday mornings during the 1960's a group of perhaps eight to ten of us used to travel the fifty miles from Dublin to Ramor on a Sunday morning, some interested in the fishing, some just happy to enjoy a nice day out in the beautiful countryside. My sister Pat, and Val's wife Coli invariably came with us and both were wonderfully imaginative gourmets and always ensured that we had superb picnics of roast chickens and cold meats, rissottos, exotic salads and bottles of wine, and the fishing would temporarily cease in the afternoon for a leisurely meal and some relaxation and laughs on the lakeshore.

Our favourite spot was on the south side of the lake, directly opposite Virginia, from where a ferry used to operate in times gone by to save people the six-mile road trek around the lake to reach the town. Here there was a lovely grassy area at the lakeside which was ideal for sunbathing and picnicking while close by there was excellent water for pike fishing, as good as anything elsewhere on the lake. Not that the lake only held pike. There were enormous shoals of big bream and many very fine trout as well, and in late May there were good hatches of mayfly that the big trout used to feed on.

A short distance up the little bohereen from the old ferry point there was a small cottage and in it lived an elderly man called Mr Gilsenan. We first met him when we called on chance to his house one day to enquire if there was anyone around from whom we could hire a boat, and he ushered us in and sat us down to have a chat. He lived alone in this quite isolated and very beautiful place and he was delighted with the company and, yes, he did have a boat which he was very happy to let us have for ten shillings a day. He loved reading, and every time we called to him to collect the oars we would bring him sheaves of magazines that he loved to read in his quiet evenings alone at home.

We quickly discovered that there were a lot of pike in Ramor and the lake was very much under fished. In those days pike were not as highly regarded as they rightly are today and the world renowned trout fisheries of the area, particularly Lough Sheelin, were the main attraction for Dublin, and indeed local, anglers. At the end of each day's fishing we would drive around the lake to the Park Hotel in Virginia to have a drink before setting off back home to Dublin. The late Barry McDonnell, who owned the hotel at the time, was a man before his time, a visionary who realised the great potential for tourism in the area if only he could interest people in coming to fish. We got to know Barry and his wife well, and our visits to the lake, and to the hotel, seemed as important to them as they were invariably enjoyable for us.

We knew very little about pike fishing at that time and certainly never considered using natural baits as might be done to day. We stuck to the good old copper spoons, kidney spoons, colorados and the odd plug, and caught lots of pike up to twelve or fourteen pounds weight either casting from the shore or trolling behind Mr. Gilsenan's boat.

Occasionally Barry used to organise a competition and ourselves, a few other visitors and the local anglers from around Virginia always very keenly contested these. On one memorable occasion, my sister Pat won the competition against all the male opposition with a handsome fifteen pounder, and we had a fantastic party in the hotel on the strength of this.

There were occasions when we were broken by a big fish and we were always subconsciously aware there was a chance that some day we might meet a really good pike.

***

One bright October Sunday Val and I arrived at the old ferry at about eleven in the morning ready for a day's fishing. There were just the two of us that day and Mr Gilsenan was not at home so, with no boat, we decided to fish from the shore.

It is a feature of Lough Ramor that on the more heavily wooded shores the trees actually grow right out into the water for several yards. We opted to fish to the east of the old ferry harbour, a particularly densely wooded section, and even though we were both wearing waders it was still quite difficult to keep clear of the trees when casting. But we liked the look of the water and knew there were plenty of pike along that shore.

I moved down past Val to a point where there was a small island about thirty yards off the shore, to the right of which was a very thick and extensive reed bed. It looked like an ideal haunt for a decent pike and I waded quietly out between the trees, took stock of the lie of the land, and started to fish.

I cast my copper spoon out several times along both sides of the island and worked it slowly and enticingly back to my feet but with no response. After maybe twenty minutes of this I decided to allow the spoon to sink for a moment or two after it hit the water, hoping that the tumbling, flashing effect might just be too much for the fish that I felt must surely live out there. So I cast it almost directly at the island, being careful not to land it into the undergrowth. I gave it a couple of seconds to sink before turning the handle and picking up the slack, visualising the spoon tumbling and flashing like a stricken fish. When I tightened up, there was an absolutely dead weight there and I cursed quietly to myself for my stupidity in probably losing yet another precious spoon. I reeled up tight and started to put some hard strain on to see could I pull it free of what I thought were the roots of a tree when to my consternation the 'dead weight' began to move. Out there near the overgrown island, something of substance had taken my spoon as it cascaded down through the dark water, and now the fish was moving inexorably away to my left, into clear water away from the sunken trees and roots.

It didn't take off in any panic but just very purposefully moved away while I applied as much pressure as I dared to try to hold it back. Val was about fifty yards further left but the

Lough Ramor pike competition, 1958
Left to right: Author, Mike Haldane, Val Demery & Dr. E. McQuade. These fine fish were all killed for the weigh-in, a practice that is now quite rightly prohibited

gentle curve of the shore and the mass of trees meant he was out of sight, so I called out to him that I was in a good fish and he shouted back a response that I couldn't quite hear. Then the fish suddenly decided that the honeymoon was over, kicked up a gear or two and shot out away from the shore in a furious run that took most of my line, and my breath, in just a few seconds. He terminated the run in a spectacular near horizontal leap, shaking his head savagely in the air before crashing back into the lake and heading off to the right, back towards the island and danger. I could see every mark on him as he made that spectacular leap and I'd almost swear that he was looking shoreward at me as he shook his head to free the copper spoon.

'*Wow, that's some fish!*' Thank God, Val was right behind me and had seen the leap. I was shaking like a leaf and my legs felt weak as all sorts of negative things were going through my head. I could picture my copper spoon, tied directly to the eight-pound nylon, with no wire trace! Although we always used a wire trace while trolling, I had deliberately decided to do without it today to make the shore casting easier. Now I could imagine the sharp teeth sawing away at the light line, see it fraying to breaking point. I could picture the pike plunging into the sunken roots and branches around the island, snagging and smashing the line like thread. But I hung on and bent the fibreglass rod near double as I tried to keep him away from the danger zone.

Make no mistake; you get tired battling with a big fish. My wrists were aching and my heart was pounding as the pike fought on. Many times I felt his tail thumping against the line as he tried to head away from the source of his annoyance and each time I waited for that awful slackness, but everything held. Eventually we could sense him tiring and we began to plan how we could get him out. In our wisdom we had neither net nor gaff and, not for the first time, we kicked ourselves that we hadn't come prepared for a really big fish.

The trees and branches growing in the water made things very difficult indeed but I managed to steer the fish about twenty yards along the shore to a spot where there were fewer of them, but there was a still a small water-worn ledge on the shoreline making it impossible to beach him. We frantically discussed our options and decided that the only chance we had was for Val to wade out as far as he could and for me to get the pike between him and the shore so that he could get two hands to him and heave him out. It was a forlorn hope but our only chance. I played the pike out until both he and I were close to exhaustion and as he began to come towards us, Val waded out into the water as far as he could. As he turned sideways in the water I compared him in my memory with the eighteen pounder from the Corrib and there was no doubt that this fish was bigger. Much bigger. His huge mottled olive flank was magnificent and his head, with my little copper spoon protruding from his jaw, was enormous. Val had also caught an eighteen pounder in the past and he was also positive that this fish was at least half as heavy again.

The fish was now between Val and I and seemed to be as quiet as he was ever likely to be. The longer he stayed in the water, the greater the risk of losing him, or so I figured. We'd never get a better chance. 'Right, Val', I said, and he reached forward and got his two hands under the pikes body, one at the shoulder and one forward of his tail and started shovelling him shoreward. For just a moment I thought that it was going to be OK, that he was ours. But as Val tried to throw the fish towards the shore, it kicked forward slightly and immediately the balance was all wrong. Suddenly frightened out of its fatigue, it turned and swam quite slowly past Val's waders and away from the shore. As the rod took the strain, there was just a little tug and the line went slack. He was gone, with my copper spoon, back towards his island haunt.

We looked at each other, we looked at the frayed end of the nylon, and we looked back at the lake. Each of us felt the loss equally badly and we waded ashore, despondent and chastened by the mistakes that had been made. No wire trace, no gaff, no net. What the hell did we expect? We simply had not anticipated meeting a fish like that while casting from the shore; we had only ourselves to blame and we knew it. We both had similar comparisons to make with our previous big pike. This was far and away the biggest either of us had ever hooked. Thirty pounds at least, we agreed, shaking our heads in silent repentance!

***

I sometimes think about that day deliberately. They are always pleasant and positive thoughts, and if for instance I'm trying to sleep, they beat counting sheep into a cocked hat! I can see again the lake and the island, and Val and the pike, and *feel* the excitement. I can, in effect, go back there, any time I like, and it will always be the same. It's of much more value to me that way than it would have been had Val and I managed to land the fish. And the pike, of course, is still out there by his island.

Quicksilver

Among anglers, you can nearly always start a lively discussion by claiming that your own favourite fish is, pound for pound, the gamest of them all. There will be instant rumblings of dissent. Pike, salmon, brown and rainbow trout will all have their champions. And there will be strident voices too, in favour of bass and mackerel from the sea, and rightly so. But in Ireland we have one native species that in my opinion beats them all and, fittingly perhaps, the sea trout is a resident of both fresh water and salt.

In my early twenties I knew nothing about sea trout other than what I had read in fishing books and magazines. I was aware that there was something special about them because, like salmon, you had to have a licence to fish for them. I read that they were wonderfully sporting fish and that sea trout fisheries were very strictly preserved. On one occasion a couple of friends and I had stopped at a bridge over a small river in west Galway to simply look at the water. Within minutes a bailiff had materialised out of nowhere and in the nicest possible way reminded us that the innocent looking river below us was a prime sea trout fishery and was definitely out of bounds to us! What was it, we wondered, that people were so jealously protecting?

My Uncle Jim, who was a very keen angler, was living in those times in Newcastle West in County Limerick. Although we both knew of our mutual interest in fishing, we had never had the opportunity to fish together. Jim fished mainly for salmon and sea trout in the south west, in Limerick and Kerry, while I fished for brown trout and some so-called coarse fish in the midlands and east, and occasionally on the Corrib.

Early one summer, out of the blue, I got a letter from Jim wondering would I like to come down and stay for a week and try the sea-trout fishing. 'And maybe with a little luck you might meet a salmon as well'. It sounded like an exciting invitation and I didn't hesitate to accept.

Now, on a lovely balmy night in July, as the headlights of the car swept across the little stone bridge over the River Feale on the Kerry-Limerick border, I was at last about to find out what these great sporting fish were all about. There was a real atmosphere of magic in the air as the car pulled off the narrow country road and the lights and engine were switched off. This was it!

Four of us got out of the car, collected our rods and bags from the boot, and started across the field towards the river. It was about 11 p.m. and even though it was July it was a cloudy, dark night. There was no glimmer of a moon, no stars, little wind and a balmy warmth in the air. A perfect night for sea trout, it was agreed.

We reached the riverside and I could see in the eternal half light of water that the river was about twenty yards wide at this point, with a very steep bank, maybe five or six feet high. We were standing at the mid point of a slow pool about a hundred yards long, and I could hear the sound of faster water downstream.

The four of us began to tackle up in the light of our flashlights. I had a ten-foot split cane rod which was apparently ideal for sea-trout and, with advice from the others, I put up a cast of three flies and was ready for action! I was pointed upstream, told that there was a nice pool about three hundred yards up there, warned to be careful of the slippery rocks where I had to wade a shallows on the way, and told to check back to base at about 3 a.m.

I set off upstream for a couple of fields until a mass of gorse growing right to the river bank materialised out of the gloom and forced me to climb down the six feet into the dark

113

water and wade carefully up along for forty or fifty yards, testing each foot as I went. When I could get out of the river again, I was at the tail of a long, glidey pool that had a narrow ledge of grass and bracken only a foot or so above the water level running along its length. The ledge was about six feet wide and then rose abruptly into a serious wilderness of briars and gorse, ten or twelve feet high, screening the pool from the fields beyond. I could just make out that there was a row of small alders running along the far bank while, apart from the tangle of briars and gorse and ferns, there were very few trees on my side. As I moved quietly along the ledge towards the head of the pool I realized that this particular spot looked ideal! I knew from my reading that sea trout preferred the quiet waters of a pool and, being very shy fish, the less accessible it was, the better. The water was dark and quite slow, the banks on both sides had lots of growth for cover and shelter and there was a quiet intimacy about the place that made you feel very much alone. As I moved further up I could see that there was quite a narrow entrance into the pool and I could hear faster water as I approached it. Suddenly, almost beside me, there was a *zzzzipp* of something in the air followed by an tremendous splash and I almost fell into the briars with the shock of it. Alfred Hitchcock would have been proud of the moment! I had just had my first encounter with a sea trout and it took a few minutes for my pounding heart to settle as the ripples spread across the river.

I waited and watched for a few minutes to let things settle down and then quietly moved on to the top of the pool. It didn't look like an easy place to fish. Behind me was the high bank of briars and gorse. Right in front of me the fast water poured into the centre of the pool, eddying gently towards my bank as I stood on the narrow ledge that was almost at water level. And fifteen yards away on the far side, almost as shadowy wraiths in the half dark, the small alders on the six foot high bank running down the length of the pool. The wicked looking tangle behind me was particularly menacing. I could visualize myself getting caught up in that and having an early ending to the night so I took out a scissors and snipped off the top dropper to leave just two flies on the cast. Then, turning back to the eerie darkness of the river, I tentatively started my sea trout career.

Taking great care I started working out some line, false casting almost parallel to the bank to avoid the briars behind me. Then, when I felt I had enough line in the air, I flicked it sideways toward the far bank, praying that I was short of the alders. After five or six casts and no problems I was getting the hang of it. As I fished on, my eyes became more accustomed to the poor light and eventually I could just about make out where the tail fly was dropping into the water. Eighty yards below me, towards the tail of the pool, another loud splash increased the heartbeat even further and I found myself concentrating on the position of the flies as I worked them across the pool and in towards the grassy ledge. Nothing. Pick up again, flick, flick, parallel to the river, then at the end of the second false cast, turn the right arm out and send the flies out at about sixty degrees to the bank. Twitch, twitch in the silence and suddenly a terrific take and somewhere out there in the darkness some wild thing is leaping and dashing, half in, half out of the water, and I'm just hanging on and hoping for the best. The suddenness of the hit and the sheer non-stop nature of the leaping completely surprised me. In five or six seconds, before I had gathered my shattered wits, it was all over and I was left standing shaking on the little ledge looking at a totally slack rod which I lifted hopefully once or twice just to make sure that the demon fish was not racing back towards me in the darkness of the river. Nothing!

What amazed me most was the frequency of the jumps, which were as complex and unexpected as an Olympic ice skater's combinations. I had the feeling that this fish had spent more time *out* of the water than in it. Ruefully, I checked the flies. OK, both still there, nothing broken and no knots or tangles. I looked back at the innocent looking pool, now quiet and peaceful again, took four or five steps downstream and started again. Flick, flick, and out to the right.

Ten or twelve casts later, almost as the flies hit the water, there was another violent commotion and a savage pull followed by a similar acrobatic series of wild leaps as a sea trout cart-wheeled his way back towards the safety of the Atlantic ocean. The fish tore yards of line off the reel in that first rush and then turned back towards my side of the river. I pulled the slack line back through the rings and let it drop around my feet as I struggled to regain some decent contact. Then away he went again in another rush towards the far bank, jumping two, three or four times as he went, before he turned and took about fifteen yards of line as he headed back for the tail of the pool again. The battle lasted maybe three or four minutes before I felt the fish tiring and I started thinking about landing him. I manoeuvred him in close to me and then, keeping the rod well up, I managed to free the landing net, slip it into the dark water and draw him over it. My first sea trout, about a pound and a half. As I looked at him in the light of the torch I was amazed that such a relatively small and slender fish could put up such a tremendous fight. Then, knees still shaking from the excitement, I checked that the cast was free of tangles and started back again.

***

Some time later, elated beyond my wildest imaginings, I looked in disbelief at my watch in the torchlight. It was almost 3.30 a.m. and I felt as if I had been here in this secret place for only an hour or so, not three or four. My cast was stuck fast in the briars behind me, not for the first time! Only this time it really was badly stuck and I had taken out the torch and felt my way in along the line to try to untangle the mess. That's when I glanced at the watch. Amid mounting panic (I had promised to be back at 3) I found the dropper and snipped it off, then did the same for the tail fly. I snipped off as much of the tangled nylon as I could find, stuffed it into my bag and set off back down the river towards the others. In my bag I had five lovely sea trout, bars of pure silver from a pound up to two-and-a-half, and I had enjoyed a more thrilling night's fishing than I ever imagined possible. In addition to the five fish I had caught, I had risen, tumbled, lost, and been totally ridiculed by maybe ten or twelve other fish. The action had been almost non-stop. And the bedlam in the pool as a mad sea trout dashed half in, half out of the water, didn't seem to upset the other residents for more that a few minutes. As long as I stayed out of the water myself there seemed to be no panic. Except, that is, for my fluttering heart. If concentration on the job were earning points that night, I would have scored twelve out of ten. It seemed that something was happening all the time, either to one of my flies or elsewhere in the pool. And it was happening all along the pool, both top, middle and bottom. Just keep the flies in the water, not in the briars, keep your concentration (not too difficult!), and be ready for anything. Literally anything! The sheer speed of these fish was bewildering, the series of five, six or seven crashing jumps in less than a couple of seconds, and then the sudden changes of direction. One minute the reel screaming as the fish heads for the tail of the pool before suddenly he's half way back again with about ten yards of slack line in a huge belly trailing after him as he jumps again, this time to say goodbye.

The other three were waiting for me when I got back to the triangular rock. Quite content, no hassle, just maybe wondering should they come and look for me. *'Any luck?'* The smiling faces were hoping for a yes! I opened the bag and in the light of a torch spilled the beautiful silver fish onto the wet grass. Three, four, five and I could sense the delight of Jim and his two friends, Charlie and Joe, and the pride they had in their lovely river. There were claps on the back, long soft whistles of approval and remarks about the pity it was that the pub was closed, as we gathered up our gear and headed happily back towards the car. I couldn't remember a better fishing experience in my lifetime than that night's.

***

During the winter that followed, Val and I tied some sea trout flies of our own, some according to traditional patterns, a few that we invented ourselves. These were often contrived, not deliberately but by accident or omission, during an attempt to tie a "standard". However, during my memorable week with Jim, Charlie and Joe I had learned a fair bit about sea trout flies both from chatting to them, from my own brief experience and from listening to the fishing talk in the pub over a nice slow pint of Arthur Guinness.

There were a couple of really dedicated fishing pubs in the south Limerick town of Abbeyfeale. These were great places, full of atmosphere. At the entrance you would find yourself in a small grocery where you could buy anything from a head of cabbage to a side of smoky bacon. Then you would push through a glass door into the next compartment, a hardware section, selling screws and nails, tools and batteries and big balls of twine, and here also was the fishing tackle. Hooks and lines, spools of nylon, and trays of wonderful salmon and sea trout flies, exquisite creations with most evocative names, tied with feathers from the four corners of the earth. Black Goldfinch, Thunder & Lightning, Dusty Miller; names that leapt out of the pages of all of the great books I had ever read about salmon and sea trout. And there they were, nestling shyly in the trays of the little shop in Abbeyfeale.

Finally, at the rear of the premises, up a couple of steps into a small bar, full of atmosphere and the lingering smell of pipe tobacco. Here you could sit with your companions and sup your pints of black stout while you poked and prodded through the trays of flies that would have been brought up from the hardware section, admiring them all, inevitably buying a few, even if only because their magnificence was totally irresistible.

***

Sitting at the fly vice that winter after my introductory week of sea trout fishing it was great fun to experiment with different materials and try to concoct something that might be totally irresistible to the fish. I felt that I knew what could be the basics for a good fly. A claret body, it had seemed, was particularly successful, and jungle cock cheeks were also especially attractive. So I 'invented' a very simple fly consisting of a body of claret seal's fur ribbed with gold tinsel, with a tail of golden pheasant tippets, a black hen hackle, starling wings and cheeks from the neck feathers of a jungle cock. As I looked at the prototype in the vice, the light making the ruby-rich seals fur glow, I did feel that it looked pretty good. Val, busily tying away on the other side of the table, squinted over his glasses at my creation and nodded his approval. That was good enough for me. A name? We had invented many flies, usually naming them after the initial vocal reaction to one of the many crises that occurred during the tying. There were 'Cock-ups' and 'Botchits' and much more dubious characters, the names of which would certainly not be found in a Hardy catalogue. But this one, with its dashing flashing jungle cock cheeks, looked the part, looked almost roguish. So I christened it *'Claret Devil'* and during the winter nights, among other patterns both good and very bad, I lovingly tied about ten of them.

***

Next year, Jim and his wife Mabel generously invited me down again for another week's fishing. Mabel was wonderfully patient and I honestly don't know how she, or my cousins Eva, Mabel, Clare and Alice, put up with us. The house became totally dedicated to fishing, the whole day revolving around the night that would follow. I was on holidays so I didn't rush out of bed in the morning but had a leisurely breakfast, a wonderful big Irish fry, cooked by Mabel and served up with the morning newspaper. Such luxury! Jim, however, was not on holidays, so despite only getting to bed at maybe 4.30 a.m. for the whole week, he had to be up and about at the normal time and off to work next morning. We usually had a good meal at about 6 p.m. before getting all the gear ready for the night ahead and when we got home again at some unearthly hour of the bright new morning, Mabel would have left us some lovely fresh sandwiches, or a plate of salads with cold meat or delicious sea trout, and the kettle was always simmering on the Aga ready to make a pot of tea. There was a pub on the way to the river where they made their own black pudding, and sometimes when we got back from the fishing we would go to Joe's house and fry the puddings with rashers and sizzling sausages to make a breakfast fit for a king.

The Claret Devil was a great hit. The problem, however, was twofold. I didn't have enough of them and they were by no means as expertly tied as those we bought in the pub. The first night I tried it I had two fish on it and so I moved it from middle dropper to the exalted position on the point. I showed it to the others and mentioned its success and to my delight they earnestly requested one each. By the end of the week they were all gone, either lost in fish or having unravelled slowly off the hooks - eaten off the hooks, I claimed!

***

I spent about four fantastic seasons down there with Jim and his friends Charlie and Joe. These two marvellous characters were both in their seventies at the time, but had an attitude and spirit that would shame any twenty year old. They would go anywhere, climb anything, try anything, and the weather mattered not a whit to them. They simply adored the river and the night fishing in particular. They both loved to fish off the big triangular rock and it was simply hilarious to watch the two of them speeding across the field to try to claim the fancied spot, half running, half walking and trying to maintain some semblance of dignity and pretend that it didn't really matter. Both of them had relatives in America and both spent a lot of time over there. I can remember one night when Charlie was flying out of Shannon at about eleven o'clock and Joe was perched on the rock looking up at the lights of a plane heading west across the blackness of the sky. 'There goes Charlie now, heading for the Catskills! And wouldn't he much prefer to be down here on this auld rock!'

I always had my own pool to myself, as the other three were quite happy to stay back at the base pool where we first came down to the river. In all the times we went there I never saw another soul on 'my' pool, except for Val. It was almost like having my own private fishery. And gradually I got to know the lie of the land much better, particularly having gone across there a few times during daylight to have a more careful look at it. Looking at it in daylight you could really see just how tight it was and how careful you had to be to avoid those briars. Unfortunately I was in them more than my fair share of times, and in the dark this could be a disaster. Patience was the key to escaping. And having a spare cast tied up in case a replacement was required.

The most memorable tangle of all time was on one occasion when Val came down for a night's fishing and came with me up to my pool. Val had spent some time in Donegal and he already knew a lot about sea trout fishing, so my main responsibility was to explain the geography of the pool to him, and to point out the hazards - the briars on our side and the alders along the far bank.

The night was good and dark and Val chose to start towards the middle of the pool while I opted for the top. We were about thirty yards apart and at that distance, against the background of the high bank, I could hardly see him at all. I called to him a couple of times to make sure he was OK and then, as usual, became completely absorbed in my own little world. Just me and the river and the sea trout. Nothing truly visible, just ghostly shadows marking the alders on the far bank. All senses concentrating on the water and the flies. Suddenly, with the usual gut-wrenching unexpectedness, a savage take almost jerking the rod away, a crashing leap out in the half dark and a good sea trout took off down the pool at high speed, my reel shrieking wildly as he went. Another crashing splash way down below followed by a distant, muffled 'Blast'(which I ignored), and then the battle assumed some sense of normality as the fish catapulted his way back up towards me. I landed him after about five or ten minutes and, hearing nothing from below me, I called 'OK Val?' The expletives that wafted back on the balmy night air were superbly chosen! My fish had performed his greatest leap about five yards out from the unsuspecting Val who thought for one ecstatic moment that he had risen the fish himself and reacted (as we all would, I soothingly told him) by striking wildly. The line, unencumbered by the weight of my three pounder, flew over his head and settled in an incredibly complex bundle in the thorny embrace of the dreaded briars.

**

For four successive years I had a magical week's sea trout fishing in north Kerry and, although we did have a few blank nights during that time, I scarcely remember them. All the memories are of wonderful nights, often fishing right through to dawn, and the fantastic *craic* I had with Jim and his friends. The climax came in the final year when we headed to the river on a Saturday afternoon to try for a salmon in a falling fresh. I can still remember the exhilaration I felt as a fish took my blue and silver devon in the centre of a streamy run, the flurry of broken water and the rush of the grilse down towards the faster water below me. It was the icing on the cake and, although the fish weighed only five pounds, it was a milestone I had often dreamed about. My first salmon! "Peter", laughed Charlie, "there's a barrel of porter for you in Abbeyfeale if you'll drink it!"

The year of the salmon was my last year sea trout fishing in north Kerry. Jim and Mabel invited me back the following year, but by then my life had taken a different direction and I no longer had the option to take time off in July. They were fantastic times, a celebration of the very best in fishing. And, if that in itself were not enough, the company of Jim, Charlie and Joe was unforgettable, and always hilarious fun. It was, quite simply, brilliant.

Winds of Change

During the summer of 1964 I began to feel very restless within myself. I felt that I needed a change and, although I had been born and reared in the suburbs of Dublin and had very much enjoyed that, I always had a nagging wish to live in the country. I felt that I would like to move to the south west and, reflecting on that now, I'm sure that the good times I had in Kerry and Limerick during the sea trout fishing with Jim must have influenced this feeling in no small way. I had been working for one of the banks since I left school so a transfer to one of their branches in the southwest should I felt, be possible. So in late summer I put in a request for a transfer which they kindly and quickly acceded to.

I was transferred to Cork city and very quickly found that it was a great place to live. The city itself was a thriving and cosmopolitan one with lots of leisure opportunities and some of the most beautiful places in Ireland very close to it. On the sea there was Cobh, Crosshaven, Kinsale and many other fabulous places, while inland there were numerous mountain ranges within a short distance, and of course a multitude of fine rivers and lakes.

I joined one of the local rugby clubs and by Christmas had bought my first car, a VW Beetle, which became my pride and joy and my passport to many adventures.

In March, when the trout season opened, I started fishing some of the smaller rivers quite close to Cork, and by April I was venturing further afield, as far north as Cahir and the Aherlow, which we had fished all those years ago. I discovered a small tributary of the Aherlow called the Arra, close to the little town of Bansha, and had some marvellous days on it during the early summer. It was a small, spring-fed river, crystal clear and with a profusion of insect life. It was perfect for dry fly and I had some really good trout up to a pound and a half from it. These fish were as plump as you could imagine, fine blocks of trout with butter-golden bellies and they fought like mad in the tiny river.

One evening in June I had an opportunity to fish the River Funcheon with a man called Jack Daly who owned a dairy farm on the banks of the river. The Funcheon is a lovely trout stream that flows into the famous Munster Blackwater not far from the town of Fermoy. It was a classic summer's evening, warm and still and bathed in golden sunshine. When I got to the farm, Jack was finishing off some of his day's chores so he pointed me towards the river and said he would join me in a half an hour.

At the waterside the air was full of insects, dancing and swirling in the evening sun. The water was summer-low and gin-clear and full of streamers of waterweed with just small gaps in between. Thinking that the fish would be taking spinners, I put up a Lunns Particular and started trying to drop it into the gaps between the streamers of weed. There were trout rising everywhere but I just could not master the situation. Either I was getting snagged in the weed or the fly dragged as soon as it hit the water. Although the river was full of good trout, catching them wasn't going to be easy.

After a short time I heard the sound of a tractor approaching and I looked up towards the top of the field that sloped gently down to the river. Over the brow of the hill came the swaying top of a fishing rod followed by Jack's head, then his shoulders and then the little red cabless tractor rocking and rolling down the grassy slope. He shut off the engine, pushed his cap back on his head and cheerfully asked how I was doing! He checked my fly, said it looked good, and reminded me it was early yet.

And then he started himself, casting with the big greenheart rod with such incredible accuracy into the little foot wide runs of clear water among the trailing strands of summer weed. Time after time, just as his fly was about to drag, a fish would dart out from the weeds to grab the fly and Jack was in one again! He must have landed about twelve decent trout of a pound to a pound and a half that he played with great skill, steering them through and over the waving strands of weed and into his waiting net. And all, except the first two, were slipped back into the water unharmed. While Jack was accomplishing all of this I rose just two trout, never hooked either of them, and got stuck in the weed a dozen times. But I did have two fine trout to take back to my landlady in Cork that night - the first two Jack had caught!

***

As the summer wore on, the old restlessness that I had felt the previous year returned to haunt me yet again. The penny began to drop that it was not a change of location that I wanted but something much more radical. At age twenty-six, after eight years working in the bank, I realised that I was no longer happy with my job, and I was more than a little frightened by this realisation. I had always been very interested in geology and during most of my school years I had intended making this my career. Now I felt that I should have followed my earlier instincts and wondered was it too late to do so now.

It was a desperately worrying time for me. Suppose I did quit my job and return to University, would I be able to handle the study? Eight years out of the system was a long time. Basics had been long forgotten, like maths and chemistry. I had done abysmally badly in my final year chemistry exams at school and was acutely aware that this was a compulsory subject in first year science at university. I had no choice; I would have to take that subject. Could I reasonably expect to improve enough to pass it? The spectre of this, and of how I could cope with the other subjects which I had never studied before at all, dismayed me.

And what about my own independence? Eight years with my own resources, and seven short months with my beloved VW, my pride and joy to which I had become so firmly attached. I would have to give that up too, and the prospect didn't appeal to me at all.

I needed some advice and lots of reassurance. My old fishing pal, Ruaidhrí, who had been through university himself, explained the entire system to me and obtained all the literature on the science faculty, college entry for mature students and everything else I would need to help me reach a decision. He was a terrific help to me, making me feel that I could handle the academic aspects of it and that, with some extra tuition, I would get through the dreaded chemistry in the first year and then have the pleasure of dropping it for good. He pointed out that my interest in geology, and indeed in the other natural sciences like zoology and botany, would give me a distinct advantage over many other students. My confidence began to rise a little.

Val too was a fountain of reassurance. As a vet he had first hand experience of college life and what it took to get through it. He emphasised that commitment was one of the key requirements. Anyone quitting a job at twenty-six to take on a four year course would only do so on the basis that they *were* totally committed. The battle is half won, he said! He also made the point that anyone who had worked for eight years was well used to the discipline of timekeeping and would therefore not be inclined to skip lectures, as would someone suddenly freed from the strict regulations of secondary school. He made it all seem easy.

My mother and stepfather, too, were also hugely reassuring. Their only concern was that I was positive that this was what I wanted to do. If so, I had their complete support.

By late September I had made up my mind to take the plunge. I applied for a place in first year science as a mature student, and got it. I was too late to make the deadline for the start of the college year but I left the bank in Cork on a Friday in late October and turned up for my first lecture as a bewildered, mature freshman on the following Monday morning.

***

Although it had its ups and downs, I thoroughly enjoyed life at University College Dublin. My younger colleagues were brilliant and accepted me straight away as just another student. Within a couple of weeks I had settled in and, to my surprise, I found that I could handle the subjects well enough to enjoy them all, even the much feared chemistry. The relief of being able to cope was enormous and I never had any reason to doubt that I would complete the course successfully.

I had surrendered my precious beetle and now had no car but this never seemed to present any real problem. Whenever I really needed a car, my dear Aunt Betty (now living in Dublin) almost pleaded with me to take her little Fiat 600, and if that weren't available, my stepbrother Brian would always come to the rescue and lend me his car for whatever the occasion was. The anticipated problem wasn't a problem at all.

Early in my second year all my lucky stars lined up for me and the course of my life changed completely. We had a demonstrator for our botany practicals who, apart from being very beautiful, was kind, considerate, extremely helpful, very interested in her subject, and overwhelmingly attractive!

During our two weekly practical classes in the botany lab I availed of every opportunity to ask for her help and finally I decided that I just had to ask her for a date. So, on the week before the Ireland versus England rugby international in February 1967, I phoned her at home and asked would she like to come to the match. To my delight and amazement she said yes, and suddenly I had a problem. I had only one ticket for the game! In those pre-corporate days it was not quite as difficult to get a ticket for an international at Lansdowne Road as it is now, but it was still not easy, and three days before a game, it was almost impossible. I blurted out the truth to her, explaining that I would try to get a second ticket and, true to form, she said she would try also. History will record that Gillian got the ticket herself and we went to the match together!

We got on very well and I soon realised that I felt much more for her than I had ever felt for anyone before. We enjoyed the same kind of things, often involving the great outdoors, and I just loved her company. She swept me right off my feet and within a year we were engaged.

***

Fishing definitely took a back seat during those days in college but there were a few memorable outings that kept my interest up. One summer, three geology student colleagues and I worked for an exploration company on a project based in Gort, County Galway. Our job involved the geological mapping of a large area close to Gort in a landscape of incredible interest. This is a classic limestone terrain and, in addition to the world famous Burren with its moonscape of bare limestone terraces and fantastic alpine flora, there were rivers which disappeared underground, lakes which temporarily dried up and mysteriously reappeared, and other fascinating features. It was like a paid holiday for us students, one of those jobs you look back on and wish you could have again.

As luck would have it, Val was then working in the town of Tuam in north Galway, and as usual was spending most of his leisure time fishing. Tuam is only about an hour from Gort and one evening I drove up there to meet him for a trout fishing session on the Clare River. This is a limestone river that flows into Lough Corrib and, as you would expect, holds some very fine brown trout that meander up from the lake. We parked the cars close to a little bridge and Val started fishing below it while I went upstream. The banks were steep, the river having been dredged many times to control the winter flooding, and it was quite tricky making one's way along the water's edge. A lot of my fishing gear was still in Dublin and we only had one net between us, and that was Val's. Déjà vu!

By about nine o'clock I had had a few takes but only from small fish and my attention was beginning to wander a bit. I was fishing down through a nice streamy run (unusual for this river) when there was an impressive bulge in the water close to where my flies were, and I caught a glimpse of a silvery back and tail, at the same time noticing the line beginning to slacken in the water. I was shocked for a moment and then I instinctively lifted the rod and felt a very solid resistance before the fish turned and fled downstream at a rate of knots, with me trying to scramble up the steep bank so I could hightail it after him. It was, of course, a salmon and my light trout rod and four pound trace were suddenly very vulnerable - to say nothing of the absence of a net and the steep bank.

For about twenty minutes I played the salmon up and down the river until he began to tire and then I started to shout for Val. It would have been funny to observe! There was I, manfully playing this salmon and screaming for Val to bring the net, and a few hundred yards further downstream, out of sight beyond the bridge, he was shouting back to me, 'Down here Polo, down here', thinking that I simply wanted to know where he was! So we were left to our own devices, the salmon and I, and to my credit, and for a change, I did it all right. I played him until he almost turned over in the water, my wrist aching with the effort, eased him in towards me and then somehow grabbed him and hugged him up the steep bank to the flat ground. He weighed almost seven pounds and was so fresh run that there were still some sea lice on him. I sauntered down to the bridge, climbed over the stiles and on down to Val. Any luck, I asked innocently, as he fished away down the stream with his back to me. He turned to say something, saw the salmon hanging from my hand, and almost fell into the river with delighted surprise.

***

Shortly after I went into my final year in college, Val went off to Kenya to work, taking with him his wife, Coli, and his three young sons. At the time it didn't occur to me that this would be a long-term post. He'd be back, I'd still be here, and we'd just pick up the fishing where we left off. But it didn't work out like that. They were gone for fifteen years and by the time they returned I was no longer living in Dublin and we never had the same opportunities to fish together as we had in the past.

***

The following summer was serious study time. In those days the final exams for a specialist science degree were held in September and I put everything else aside to work as hard as I could. The reservoir at Roundwood was a tremendous release from all the pressures when things got a bit too much.

I could jump into a borrowed car and within forty minutes be strolling across a field to the water feeling as though I were on another planet. Sit down on the stump of a tree and watch the sun dropping as the first murragh hatches and the trout start to feed. Then wade in and start to cast and you are lost again in a world of your own where nothing can disturb you. The ultimate tonic for anything.

On one of these escapes I had the best evening's fishing that I had ever had on the reservoir. It was a warm, dark evening with a touch of gentle, misty rain in the air and there was a very good hatch of the big sedges. Trout began to feed and soon were working their way into the shallows after the scurrying flies, slashing and boiling under them with fierce gusto. In an hour and a half I had six fine trout, the best a beauty of two and a half pounds, and I had missed at least the same number. It was wonderful shore fishing and the best possible way to recharge the batteries for the following day's graft at the books.

In September I sat my final exams and a couple of weeks later learned that I had been awarded an honours degree in geology. The gamble had worked! Three days after the results were posted Gillian and I were married and a few weeks later the two of us headed off to a gold mine in the Western Transvaal of South Africa to my first job as a geologist. It was November, early summer in southern Africa, and soon the temperatures began to soar. Occasionally at lunchtime I used to drive the short distance to the Vaal River, which formed the provincial border with what was then called the Orange Free State. I would park in the shade of the towering bridge which carried the road and railway across the river and watch the swirling, turbid water flow westward towards its meeting with the Orange River before heading on towards the south Atlantic. A huge river, well over 1,000 miles from its source in the Drakensberg Mountains of Eastern Transvaal, to the sea. I used to watch the swallows, beautiful acrobatic creatures, swooping around and beneath the massive bridge, and wonder how such delicate birds could migrate all the way back to Europe, some of them to Ireland, to nest. In the source waters of the river, way up in the Drakensberg Mountains, there was good trout fishing I was told. But here, on the flat lands of the high veldt, the sluggish red water held only catfish, enormous flaccid creatures with fleshy whisker-like barbels growing from the sides of their mouths. I wasn't interested, and played golf instead.

***

That Christmas, as always, I sent John Joyce a card. As I wrote it on the *stoep* in the heat of South Africa's summer I imagined what it must be like then on the windswept shores of the Corrib; or sitting round the turf fire in John's cottage with maybe a drop of poitín to keep out the winter's cold. Some months later I received an unexpected letter from home with the sad news that John had died just a few weeks before Christmas. As I sat and read it, over and over again, I thought of the last time Gillian and I had seen him; the stories and *craic* in Jim Egan's bar and the bottle of stout and 7-Up for the journey back to Gort. He was an irreplaceable character and I felt a huge loss that I wouldn't see him again.

Tipperary!

Eighteen months later Gillian and I, with our new baby daughter, Stephanie, were back in Ireland. I had done what most new graduates had to do, which was to spend a year or so abroad for work experience before tackling the job market at home.

We were very lucky in our timing. A new era of mining had begun in Ireland in the middle '60's with the discovery and development of the Tynagh lead-zinc ore body near Loughrea, and suddenly there were prospectors working all over the country looking for other mineral deposits. The Tynagh discovery had been an encouraging factor in my decision to give up my job in the bank and study for a degree in geology. I could see opportunities for work as a mining geologist rather than in the fields of academia or research that were not of particular interest to me. Years earlier, our school geography textbook had stated quite flatly that there were no economic mineral deposits in Ireland. Now, thanks to the expertise, inspiration, and dedication of a few entrepreneurial Irish geologists who had returned from the mines of Canada, some remarkable discoveries were made which placed Ireland onto the world's mining map in a big way.

After Tynagh, further mineable zinc-lead ore bodies were discovered at Silvermines in Co. Tipperary and these too were developed into a mine. Copper was discovered at Gortdrum, also in Tipperary, and this also became a mine. And in addition there were many sub-economic finds, sustaining the high level of prospecting interest which culminated in the discovery in the early '70's of the massive zinc-lead deposits at Navan, Co. Meath and, later in the '90's, two more zinc mines at Galmoy,

Co. Kilkenny and at Lisheen, Co. Tipperary. It was definitely a good time to be a geologist.

So it was that in early 1971 we were back in Ireland, not in Dublin, but in County Tipperary, about to start working at the Mogul zinc mine at Silvermines near Nenagh. I knew very little about the area. Nenagh was a fine market town on the road from Dublin to Limerick and I was aware that one of the big Shannon lakes, Lough Derg, was close by but had never heard it talked about as a classic trout fishery in the same revered sense as Sheelin, Corrib or Mask.

We rented a lovely timber bungalow on the shores of the lake at a place called Youghal Bay. The picture window looked right out across the half-mile wide bay towards the wooded shore around Youghal Quay. There was a little harbour at the bottom of our garden, and the rent for the house included a good lake boat and a 6 horsepower outboard engine.

We realised just how big the lake was very early on, when we drove along the Killaloe road from Portroe and stopped at a place aptly called 'The Look Out'. From this high ground we could see right across the lake towards Scarriff on the Clare side and northwards, away beyond the large island of Islanmore, towards Portumna in Co. Galway, twenty miles away. It was a wild, stormy February day, and Lough Derg looked dark and grey and threatening, with a steady line of big waves marching up from Killaloe. I couldn't equate it in my mind with Corrib or Sheelin, it looked too enormous, too exposed and featureless on this cold winter's day, to be a lake really suitable for trout.

***

From the fishing point, my thoughts seemed to turn naturally towards the nearby Nenagh River, a gorgeous trout stream rising in the hills around Templederry and flowing into Lough Derg at Dromineer bay. The nicest stretch of the river was just a few miles from where we lived and, as luck would have it, there was a little thatched pub close by, run by the late and incomparable Nell and Bill Kennedy, where we quickly got to know a lot of people in the warmest of atmospheres. From the outset we were made to feel at home and very welcome and somehow I knew straight away that I was going to really enjoy my time in Nenagh.

That spring I fished wet flies, getting to know some lovely stretches of the river below Ballyartella Bridge, and after South Africa it was great to be back fishing again. As the weather warmed up I began to fish dry flies and by early May I had discovered a little spent-tied fly which the trout seemed to take when the spinners of the blue winged olive were on the water in the evenings. I was perfectly content on the river but as May approached, the fishing talk in Nell and Bill's began to switch to the mayfly.

By this time I had ventured out a few times in the boat. On one afternoon in early April I had trolled quietly up along the shore on our side of the bay and I had a nice trout of just under two pounds on a small mepps. But most of the time we used the boat simply for pleasure, mooching around Youghal Bay and not really venturing beyond that into the wider reaches of the lake beyond Rinskaheen Point.

Early in May we saw our first mayfly fluttering across the garden into the hawthorn bushes, and by the 10th or 11th of the month we were seeing good hatches of fine big flies in the reeds outside our little harbour. The penny still refused to drop and I still failed to recognise the lake as a prime trout fishery like the other great limestone lakes. There were very few boats about, so I concluded that the fishing couldn't be all that great. I can remember one Sunday driving down a bohereen to a little quay further up the lake. It was another wild, wet day with grey skies and slanting rain, and very cold for May. The lake looked like a sea and you could hardly make out the far side in the driving rain and mist. Sitting in the comfort of the car, we watched a boat with three men, dapping rods almost horizontal in the gale, as they drifted along about thirty yards off the shore. Hoods pulled over their heads, backs to the driving rain, they looked frozen and soaked and the man on the oar was having to work really hard to keep some control of the drift as the boat sped past. I looked around out of curiosity and made out three other boats in the expanse of lake that I could see. If this were the Corrib there would have been so many more at mayfly time.

**

During the week that followed the weather improved greatly. The harsh, cold wind eased, temperatures rose and we got some real summer-like May days. The lake now looked beautiful, the temptation too great to ignore, so one evening I asked Gillian to pick me some mayflies the following day while I was at the mine, and promised myself a few drifts after work.

I spent two glorious evenings on the lake and, although there were good hatches of mayfly, I never saw a trout. In truth, the prevailing southwest wind was all wrong for Youghal Bay and I didn't make any attempt to go further afield where I might have found a more suitable drift. I was content to just enjoy the couple of hours. So I gave up on it each evening at about 7.30 and came ashore for my dinner. It was back to the river for me.

**

About ten days later, towards the very end of May, we got one of those hot, sultry, almost thundery days, so typical of early summer heat waves. When I got home from work a fantastic sight met me. Hordes of dancing mayfly gnats everywhere. Every tree, every bush had its own population, rising and falling in a wonderful, pulsing rhythm. And to add to the profusion, clouds of tiny midges, millions of them, like smoke over the tops of some of the trees. I had never seen such an extravagance of insect life before, not even in the heady days of Sheelin. This tiny patch of shoreline, this microcosm within the enormity of the entire lake, contained so many flying creatures that the mind boggled at the thought of this happening right around the vast shoreline. At the bottom of the garden, the empty boat beckoned to me from the little harbour and beyond it I could see the hazy, shimmering flat calm of the lake. I had to have a look.

I rummaged through my dry flies and found a battered gnat that had survived Lough Sheelin days and within ten minutes I pushed the boat out through the reeds outside the harbour. I could see quite a few dead male gnats on the water and females were already making their way out to lay their eggs. There were no Green Drakes about, the hatches had finished quite a few days before, but there were plenty of small brown sedges in addition to the male gnats. I sat in the boat maybe twenty yards off the shore, right out from the house, and watched. Below me in the water I could see the huge, round boulders of limestone that characterise this part of the Tomona shore and I wondered what gargantuan pike must haunt those reedy depths. The combination of heat, birdsong, droning insects, and the soothing lapping of water against the boat, was almost narcotic and I felt my eyes closing in the soothing comfort of it all.

From the corner of a sleepy eye I saw a dimply movement in the water between the shore and me. Very quiet, very tiny. And another. *Perch, there must be a shoal of perch, this lake is full of them.* I sat up and watched. Another dimpling rise, close to the first one. The few gnats and brown sedges on the water were enough to interest a fish, no doubt about it. *Would perch take a fly?* Bream would, I knew that. Fully alert again, I picked up the fly rod, detached the battered gnat from the cork handle and gave it a dab of silicone. Another dimple, very close to the shore, quiet and hardly disturbing the flat calm water. I pulled a few yards of line off the reel and began to false cast, working about ten yards out and dropping the gnat in the general direction of the last dimple. The spent-tied gnat with its battered hackle sat well down in the film, very difficult to see. I was concentrating now, fully alert and interested, tense almost. Something was happening here, I was beginning to feel more certain.

I swung my eyes to another dimple five yards to the right, and then quickly back to my own fly. *Can't see the damn thing at all now.* A dimple very close to where it must be. *Come on, perch! Take it!* Then, *Bloody Nora, is that my cast moving?* In my surprise I'm sure I said the words aloud. Panic, tighten up into something very solid indeed, accompanied by a tremendous surge in the flat calm water and a mighty thump on the rod. Immediately, that awful slackness of nothing. For a few seconds the little boat rocked as I stumbled on my feet to regain my balance and looked in astonishment at the spot near the reeds. It looked so innocent with just a cluster of bubbles on the surface. I looked around me, for reassurance almost. Not another boat in sight in the sleepy calm of the bay. Dismayed, I reeled slowly in, knowing what I would find. The gnat was gone, the six-pound nylon cleanly broken at the knot.

There must have been a damn good trout in among those perch! I frantically searched through my boxes for another gnat and in among the collection of useless, gaudy mayflies collected over the years I found another one. Bigger, very dark and heavily hackled, it would have to do. I tied it on, making doubly sure this time to wet the nylon before I pulled the knot tight, and started watching again. Another dimple about twenty yards further up the shore, so I paddled quietly within range and threw the gnat out. I could see immediately that I was wasting my time. The big bushy fly stood out like a sore thumb among the delicate real things and quite clearly nothing would be foolish enough to look at it twice. I gave it half an hour and then pulled ruefully back to the little harbour to tell Gillian of my adventure.

＊

That evening virtually saw the last of the gnats going out and the mayfly was over for the year. Looking across the bay that evening I wondered just what I had missed by ignoring the lake at a time when I had a boat and an engine sitting idle at the bottom of the garden, just waiting to be pushed out.

I fished away on the river for the remainder of that season. As the summer wore on, most of the other anglers fished wet flies and came in with much better trout that I was catching on my little spent dry flies, but I was having fun. There is a long, slow moving, almost canal-like reach above Ballyartella bridge known as 'The Flat', a favourite spot for the wet fly anglers, while I preferred the more varied water away below the bridge that suited the dry fly better. Late one night, Con Corrigan, one of the anglers who regularly fished The Flat, came in to the pub in Ballycommon with a very happy expression on his beaming face, and called for a pint. We looked curiously at the plastic bag he was carrying and asked had he any luck. Just one, he laughed, and he opened the bag and out tumbled a wonderful brown trout that weighed almost six pounds. Amazingly, on each of the following two nights Con brought in another big trout, each between five and six pounds and in perfect condition. Three in a row. Big strong fish with tails like spades, straight up from the lake, and all caught after dark at the top of The Flat on a lake-sized Golden Olive. Mighty fish anywhere, but from a river, absolutely outstanding.

＊

Dromineer Castle, Lough Derg, mid 1970's
Evening reflections.

By October baby Stephanie was fifteen months old and beginning to get her feet under her, and Gillian and I decided that the lakeside bungalow was no longer safe for her. The little harbour at the bottom of the garden had about two feet of water in it and the risk of an accident was not acceptable. So we found another house and said goodbye to the stunning view that we had enjoyed across Youghal Bay. It had been such a pleasure to live there among the coots and moorhens, the grebes and swans, and to walk through the fields late in the evening, picking mushrooms and blackberries, or just enjoying the perfect peace of the place.

Lough Derg

The River Shannon is the longest river in Ireland, rising in County Cavan in the north west of the country, and making its way southward for one hundred and sixty miles to the ancient city of Limerick. With its eleven hundred miles of tributaries, it has a catchment area of six thousand square miles, and drains about one fifth of the entire island of Ireland.

There are three major lakes on the Shannon: Lough Allen, Lough Ree, and Lough Derg, the lowermost one, which borders on the counties of Galway, Clare and Tipperary. Lough Derg is about twenty-four miles long with a total area of fifty square miles and there are numerous islands on it, the largest of which is Islanmore (*Oileann Mor*, the large island), mid-way along the lake.

It is a lake of many moods, and it is wise to respect them. On a still, sunny evening in summer it can be as docile and serene as a millpond, and unimaginably beautiful. To look across the stillness of the lake on a summer's evening towards an orange sun setting behind the hills of Clare is like living in a picture postcard. But when the gales blow from the southwest, straight up the lake from Killaloe, it's another story, with big rolling waves capped by ragged white horses that trail their misty spray away up wind like rain. When it's like this, the sensible thing to do is stay off the lake until it quietens down again.

***

Our second May in Nenagh saw my real introduction to Lough Derg. George Herriott, a good fishing friend from the river, had asked me several times the previous year to come and fish the mayfly on the lake. Now, on this second season, George brought the subject up again and this time I was more than keen to take up his offer. The following morning at the little boathouse in Dromineer I met George and his brother Michael, home from England for his never missed fortnight's fishing, and thus began a great friendship that has lasted ever since. It was what you could describe as a good fishing day, with a strong, steady breeze from the southwest and some glimpses of early summer sun through plenty of white cumulus, and pleasantly mild, even on the lake. Good dapping weather. Mayflies were already hatching among the reeds close to the pier as we loaded our gear into the boat and we were full of anticipation as we pushed out and started the engine.

***

As we motored out into Dromineer Bay that morning we made our plans for the first part of the day. A couple of drifts across the Corrikeen islands and then, having confirmed the steady south west breeze, we intended heading into Urra Point for a drift along the Urra shore, across Nellies Angle and into the back of Luska Bay.

There was now a good steady hatch going on and we were soon dapping across the inside point of the Corrikeens, without seeing a fish. One more drift there, and we made for the Urra shore. Michael was on the oar, and soon we were following a couple of good looking lines of fly down along the beautifully wooded shoreline. Both he and George seemed to see *everything* that moved in the water all around the boat. They seemed to be able to watch their own flies and keep an eye on the wider scene, sometimes pulling the boat ten or fifteen yards to one side to cover a rise and then returning to the main line. I couldn't see half of what they pointed out to me.

Within half an hour or so Michael said quietly, *'Peter, there's a rise twenty yards ahead of you'*. I had seen nothing but I could feel the adrenalin pumping hard as I tried to keep the fly down on the water. Little gremlins of wind seemed determined to whisk it away. The more I concentrated the more it took on a life of its own, but through all the shaking and twitching I managed to keep it down. *'We're almost on him now'*, George this time, very matter of fact! Steady, steady! And suddenly, a lovely, swirling take and my dap was gone. I lowered the rod, waited a couple of seconds, and struck quite hard. The line was well down, always a good sign, and sure enough I was in a fish. God bless John Joyce, and Petey Tierney! I coaxed him round the bow and after a couple of minutes he slid over the net and was hoisted into the boat. A lovely two pounder, a typical shore fish, short and deep with beautiful markings; a real wild Shannon trout. I sensed immediately that the three of us were equally delighted. It was a fish in the boat, our collective success, and a fine start to the day.

We had good fishing for most of that day and eventually I got my eye in and began to see more of what was going on around us. I was impressed by the way George and Michael selected their drifts with great care and kept the boat firmly on line as it drifted down the wind. Sometimes they would see that an adjacent line had a better 'trickle of flies' going down it and the boat would be easily manoeuvred so that one of the daps covered that line. And if Michael were playing a fish, George would shift the oar quietly to the stern pin and keep the boat faithfully on the chosen drift. All done very comfortably, with no fuss and no missed fishing opportunities.

At about four o'clock we filled the old smoke-blackened kettle with lake water and pulled into one of the traditional landing sites for grub. In a sheltered spot among the trees and gorse bushes, we lit a fire of sticks in a hearth made of limestone rocks that has been used by anglers for hundreds of years. As though the smoke were a signal, another boat joined us, and then another, and soon there were eight or nine of us enjoying our grub and discussing the results of the morning. Then, without much delay, out on the lake again and another drift, this time along the east side of Cameron Island. Another couple of nice fish and by now the hatches were nearly finished, just an odd fly here and there. But we stayed on out there until about nine o'clock, half an hour or so after we had seen the last rise, and my hands and feet were thoroughly frozen by then. Remember this in future, I thought. Bring plenty of warm gear, even if you never have to use it.

The light was fading as we got back into Dromineer where Margaret, the inexhaustibly patient caretaker of the boat club, was there as always to check us safely ashore. We pulled up the boat and put the engine away before ambling up to the warmth of the little pub for a couple of well earned pints. Inside, other anglers, lots of stories and dramas of the day, opinions on the probable weather for tomorrow, and all the usual magic atmosphere of a typical fisherman's pub.

Another two days with Michael and George left me totally captivated by Lough Derg, and the following year I took a week's holiday for the mayfly and have done ever since, missing only two years in the intervening twenty five.

***

One of the first days I was on Lough Derg I was with George and his uncle, Al. At that stage Al had been fishing the lake every May, without fail, for about fifty years, and he knew every feature of it, every haunt where a decent fish might be found. We were dapping the mayfly over on the Clare side, between Williamstown and Hare Island, on a good fishing day of alternating sunshine and light showers, and a nice lively breeze from the north east. There was a good hatch of fly going on and there was a collective sense of expectation in the boat as we neared the rocky point of Samson's Bay.

'There's always a decent fish here', Al commented, as we got within thirty yards of the point, and an interested observer might have noticed George and me leaning forward in our seats in anticipation! You could see why Al expected a good fish. The prevailing southwest winds carry all the surface flotsam from the whole Bunlachy shore up past this shallow, rocky point. It is a feeding station that you would expect to be jealously guarded against all intruders by a very classy fish indeed.

The conversation petered out as we approached the point itself where the little bright yellow gorse bushes clung to the fractures among the chaotic blocks of limestone. In the silence, the bubbling song of unseen skylarks seemed to fill the air and each of us was effectively alone with just his own thoughts of what might lie in ambush only a few yards away. Hearts were beating fast.

I was at the stern of the boat and my dap would be the closest to the rocks. I was convinced Al was right; there would be a big fish here. My concentration was such that I almost had a dead man's grip on the rod, struggling to present the dap properly, to keep it on the water without skittering it about, or worse still, lifting it into the air at just the wrong moment.

George had the boat on a perfect drift, and as we passed within an oar's length of the rocks there was a nice bulge under my fly followed by a solid swirling eddy, like a stroke from a frogman's flipper, and that was it. The fly twirled giddily on the surface in the centre of the dissipating swirl, untouched and rejected. I thought of John Joyce and the fish that came back for the grasshopper. *Leave it to him, leave it to him.* But I knew this one wouldn't come back. 'He missed it', said George sympathetically, being more than reasonable with me. But we both knew he hadn't; something had been wrong with the presentation and he just didn't like what he had seen.

Everything had looked so perfect. Good wave, nice sunshine and shade of a typical Irish sky in springtime - any shadows cast by boat or rod were behind us with the wind from the northeast. Mind you, the cast did glint a little in the sun. *The cast!* With growing suspicion and horror I looked at it again. I followed it with my eye from the floss blow line to where it ran into the water about eight or ten inches *ahead* of the fly, the far side of the fly. The only object on the water should be the dap itself, definitely not twelve inches of the nylon cast. In my anxiety to keep the fly steady on the water I had made the fatal error of allowing the tip of the cast to sink, and of course it bellied out ahead of the dap as you would expect. The trout must have seen the cast glinting in the wavelets as it rose to take the fly; or maybe even bumped it with its nose. And, like the decent fish he was, he became alarmed and shied away, leaving that tantalising swirl as he hid among the massive boulders passing silently beneath the gently rocking boat.

Perhaps he wasn't a big fish, and we certainly couldn't be sure because we never saw him. But he was definitely in the right place to be a good one, and the displacement of water as he turned away from the fly was very impressive indeed. But like the Lough Ramor pike, the fact that we didn't catch him seems to add to the enduring nature of the moment, and often when we drift again across that point I find myself lost in thoughts of the good things of that day. The rounded cloud shadows on the green foothills of the Arra mountains; the gorse blossom, blazing yellow in the sunshine; the mayflies sailing along in the breeze; and the lyrical, bubbling sweetness of the skylarks. In particular, it reminds me of Al, of the many great days we enjoyed fishing with him, and the wealth of wonderful stories he told about the lake. He was an extraordinary man, a role model for us all, fishing the mayfly on Lough Derg until he was ninety two, and loving every precious moment of it.

***

Fishing on Derg is not easy; you have to be patient, prepared for the long haul, and ready to take the limited chances that come your way. Even during the strongest of mayfly hatches it can be very frustrating to find that there are few fish feeding on the surface. There is an incredible richness of feeding on the lake bottom and that's where the trout are to be found except in unusual circumstances. Although there may be thousands of mayfly sailing along during these big hatches, the activity of the nymphs at or close to the bottom must be incredible altogether. So one fish feeding on the surface, *looking up,* as Michael aptly puts it, is worth ten thousand feeding on the bottom. He is the catcheable fish.

It took me a while to realise the importance of this. I had often seen Michael or George manoeuvre the boat short distances to cover a fish that had risen to one side of the drift. But I was genuinely amazed at their persistence in actually reeling in to row back maybe a hundred yards, and come again over a fish which we had obviously already covered, evidently not to perfection, but nevertheless with a high degree of certainty. There had never been a need for such persistence on the Corrib - if you just carried on there would be another trout feeding on the surface not too far down the drift.

There was one outstanding example of this. It was a very cold and miserable morning with a stiff half gale from the south, and driving, heavy showers soaking everything in the boat. We spent several hours drifting the east shore of Islanmore, struggling both to keep the flies on the water and our spirits up, until thankfully Michael filled the kettle and I knew that some temporary relief was at hand. We pulled ashore and soon had a decent fire going and the kettle on the boil for mugs of much needed tea. I suffer from poor circulation and my fingers were frozen and white with the cold. My feet were also perished and my overriding thought was that it would be grand to be somewhere else, anywhere, but preferably by a nice turf fire with a pint of Guinness and a Hamlet cigar.

I wrapped my petrified fingers around a mug of scalding tea and watched the steaks sizzling on the grill as the circulation returned. Huddled under the hood of my oilskin, I looked across the choppy water towards Islanbrien and gradually began to feel that, maybe after all, I could keep going for a few more hours.

We stayed around the embers of the dying fire for longer than usual and at about five o'clock we decided to push out again into the wind and rain. As we beat our way slowly up along the shore of Islanmore, waves breaking over the bow and thumping into the back of my oilskins, I wondered again was there any faint hope that Michael would say, *Sin a bhuill*, let's head for home.

We crossed the shallows to Islanbrien, turned the boat sideways to the wind, and managed, despite the numb fingers, to put up a couple of fresh daps. There was a nice hatch going on and the flies were finding it difficult to get off the water in the strong wind so there was a good line of battered looking mayfly going down in front of us as we started the drift tight to the shore.

The wind was perfect, the foam lines running out in front of us precisely parallel to the shore. Michael had the stern in shoreward so that he could keep the boat on the preferred drift by pulling forward on the trailing oar, and in the howling wind he was having to work really hard. I sat in the stern, trying to concentrate, struggling to keep the dap from either drowning or from flapping uselessly in the air. It was brutal, and as my hands got wet and frozen again it was almost impossible to be interested.

About a hundred yards down the drift there was a small indentation in the rocky shore, maybe about twenty yards long and ten yards deep. As we passed the top of it Michael shouted, *'There's a rise'*, and gestured towards the far end of the little inlet. I saw nothing, but being on the inside, closest to where Michael had indicated, my concentration was suddenly up a few notches again despite the bitter cold. We seemed to shoot past the inlet and I saw Michael reel in. *'We'll have to cover him again'*, he shouted as he took the strain on the oars. I managed to catch my flailing dap and sat tight as Michael pulled the boat away from the shore, waves breaking green over the side, and then turned back into the half gale to get above the fish again. Fifty yards above the little nook, out went the two daps again and we drifted fast down the wind towards the inlet. As we drew level with it I saw a good aggressive rise about five yards in from the line of our drift. It was impossible in the wind to get the dap in far enough to cover the fish as the near side of the inlet was guarded by a couple of big rocks over which the waves were breaking hard. Michael saw it too and as we cleared the lower end of the inlet he reeled in again and pulled out to start back to the top again. As we started the drift this time, he left his own rod inboard to concentrate on trying to get the boat, and my fly, as close to the fish as possible. He skilfully brought us close to the two rocks, and holding the rod almost at arm's length in the fierce wind, I got the dap a few yards inside the line of the boat, close to where the trout had last shown. Another splashing rise, behind and inside the boat, signalled that we had failed to cover him again, and I expected Michael to call it quits and carry on down the drift. But he didn't. He pulled back again into the wind and driving rain, five times in all, until finally my battered dap disappeared in a good confident take.

It was obvious that he was a good fish and that we were in a tough spot, wild water and wicked rocks everywhere, but Michael managed to keep the boat from galloping away down the wind and after ten minutes we had him in the net. He was a fine fish, well over four pounds, and suddenly the cold and the wet didn't seem to matter so much. I knew by looking at the fish that it was probably the heaviest trout of my career so far. When I thought of how hard Michael had worked to enable me to catch the fish, I felt a bit like a piece of cargo! But as he pulled us away from the shore towards deeper water, Michael shook his head and grinned, *'He was looking up!'*

***

To give yourself the best chance of success on Lough Derg, it is also very important to focus on the correct line, the place where an interested fish is most likely to be. On a day with a decent fishing breeze, lines of foam will form parallel to the wind, and on these the flotsam collects and a surface-feeding trout will concentrate. These lines are generated by wave, wind and convection, and can originate at a headland, the point of an island or even a big rock over which the waves are breaking.

On one particular day when Michael and I were out together, the wind was again from the south and we did a few drifts along the top end of the Urra shore which suits this wind, but for a long time we saw nothing. When we reached the point where the shoreline curves gently to the north east, the foam lines ran away outwards from the shore towards the Buggane Island about a mile away. We followed the main line out towards this island, knowing that it was all good shallow water, nowhere more than ten or twelve feet deep. There were a few flies going down the line and although we continued for maybe half a mile towards the island, we saw no sign of a rise.

We pulled back to the shore again and this time nosed into a small reed bed from which a less prominent foam line originated some thirty or forty yards to the right of the main line. There was a hatch going on right inside us in the reeds and the newly hatched flies were being carried out along this one particular line only.

We followed the line out, covering both sides of it with our daps, and within fifty yards we met our first fish. He rose a few yards in front of us, taking a mayfly in typically aggressive form, and then boned Michael's fly down without any hesitation. We saw another two fish on the same drift before we decided that we had gone far enough and pulled back to the reeds to do it again.

We had a fantastic two hour's fishing on that line, seeing activity every time we did the drift. Michael had three fish and I had two, all between two and three pounds, and we must have missed about the same number again. We knew for sure we were in the right place because two other boats, seeing what was happening, started the drifts on either side of us. One was maybe fifty yards to one side, the other a little further away on the other. Neither of these boats rose a fish and it was obvious to us that the only correct line was the one coming off the little reed bed where the mayflies were actually hatching. Such a small difference, but so important. When the hatch ended, so did the fishing, but we had a field day while it lasted.

***

We also discovered that very often the most likely place to meet a trout is right in on the rocks along the shore, almost up on the grass it seemed. The first time we realised the importance of this was late one year when the hatches were almost finished in the upper part of the lake that we usually fished. So, as much for the sightseeing as the fishing, we headed off down the lake, past Youghal Bay and Parkers Point and on to the Scilly Island at the top end of the deep channel that runs down to Killaloe. We had never fished beyond Scarriff Bay before and knew nothing about the area, but we noticed a few mayflies hatching on the south side of the island and decided to give it a go. We did a drift along one side of the island and then decided to fish straight in to the south shore of it. There was a fairly stiff breeze blowing and as we got to within about ten yards of the shore we reeled up and pulled back out to start again, having seen nothing. We did the drift again and this time we decided that one of us would fish it right onto the rocks while the other reeled in and had the oars ready to pull the boat away at the last minute. I had the privilege of fishing out that first drift and, sure enough, as the dap was about to beach itself on the rocks, there was a confident, leisurely rise and we were in business! We had great sport that day, doing short drifts straight into the island from a couple of hundred yards out. Every fish we had, we got within a few feet of the shore, and one of them was a lovely four pounder that fought like a demon among the rocks in just a few inches of water. If you were on your own in the boat there is no way you could do it. Even if you did manage to fish it out, you could not play a decent fish and manoeuvre the drifting boat away from the shore at the same time.

We had a similar incident a year or two later when we were drifting into the reeds at the back of Luska Bay. As we approached the reeds and thought about reeling in we could see that, behind the first couple of feet of reeds, there was a small patch of clear water just a few yards wide. Michael was elected to fish it out while I reeled in and got the oars ready to pull us clear at the last minute. When the time came, he lifted the dap over the first row of reeds and dropped it neatly into the clear water behind, and almost immediately a good trout performed the most awesome, slow motion rise you could imagine. His entire head and shoulder seemed to emerge vertically out of the water under the fly, and then simply subside again, taking Michael's dap with him. No forward movement whatsoever. There was hardly a ripple on the surface as he performed this feat, and there wasn't a word from either of us as the water closed quietly over his disappearing head. Despite his astonishment, Michael duly lowered the rod for a moment or two and then tightened up into a fine fish that must have felt very secure in his haven behind the rampart of reeds.

***

We discovered the value of good sustaining food at quite an early stage. From eleven in the morning until ten o'clock at night is a long session on the lake, particularly in cold weather, and the value of proper eating cannot be overstated. In the early days we used to bring out the usual assortment of sandwiches, sardines, cheese and biscuits. All cold things, except for the tea we made. By early evening you could feel the stamina disappearing through the soles of your boots. Even with a flask of coffee, or of the nourishing homemade nettle soup that Michaels's sister, Toni, often made for us, it was tough going from then to the end of the day.

One day we were ashore on an island having our lunch and trying to keep warm and dry. It was a raw, windy day and the morning and early afternoon had been long and hard with no fish to show for it. A few hundred yards up the shore another boat had pulled in and two other anglers were taking their break, brewing up their tea on their fire. As we chewed on our cold sandwiches, the unmistakable aroma of frying steak came drifting along on the breeze, and it was so appetising. We were like the Bisto kids as we followed the smell along the shore towards the other fire to see what was going on. The two men were sitting comfortably, each on a nice flat-topped rock, eating big slices of well-buttered brown bread and drinking mugs of tea, while two fine T-bone steaks sizzled on a big, black frying pan in front of them. Michael took one look and made his mind up. From that day on, this was going to be us. The following morning he located the gridiron off an old cooker, bought some steaks, and we had a meal fit for three kings when we pulled ashore. A season or two later, Michael introduced the idea of having hot soup as a starter, heated in an old pressure cooker that he had found at home. The result was a longer, much more restful break, hot and delicious food, and buckets more stamina. A cup of hot coffee from a flask at about seven or eight o'clock, and there was no problem lasting through until ten o'clock at night.

It has to be stressed that the lighting of fires is strictly forbidden in most parts of Ireland's countryside. On the big lakes, however, like Corrib, Mask and Derg, anglers have been boiling kettles on open fires for donkey's years, the fires being lit in one of many traditional hearths made of the local limestone rocks. These fires are always strictly supervised and totally extinguished before the anglers depart.

***

Although we had some tremendous fishing on the dap during the first couple of years that I fished with George and Michael, we realised that we were missing out on something. There were hours, even days, when the breeze failed to blow and the surface of the lake was calm and still and beautiful, but the dap just would not go out. Those days were spent patiently waiting for any little zephyr of wind that might allow an hour or two's dapping, or in mooching around in the boat enjoying the fine weather and the sights and sounds of the lake. Sometimes we would fish wet flies, usually mayfly nymphs, but we were really interested in the fish that were feeding on the hatched insects on the surface.

There was another big disadvantage to dapping, even when the breeze was kind to us. Being totally wind-dependent, it was impossible to cover a fish that rose to one side of the boat or, worse still, upwind of it. While the dap would only fish downwind, a dry fly could be cast in any direction, even back up the drift into the wind.

Most of the other anglers on the lake were in the same predicament as ourselves but there were some notable exceptions, very skilful dry fly anglers who could find suitable water to fish in almost any weather, and who caught some tremendous fish, particularly on the spent gnat.

It was only a matter of time before we, too, started to bring the dry fly rods with us.

Spent Gnat

It was eight thirty on a fine evening in May and three of us were drifting along the Bunlachy shore on the Clare side of Lough Derg. It had been a thoroughly good dapping day and we had several nice fish in the boat, including one beautifully marked five pounder taken from the rocks around the wild little islands of Bunlachy where the black headed gulls nest, screeching their resentment at every passing boat.

The hatches were over for the day, the breeze had died, and in the evening sunlight we could see the mayfly spinners, the gnats, going out overhead, and quite a few of them already spread-eagled on the water. We were dapping away in the light air, still confident that there was another fish to be had before we reeled in for the day and headed home for Dromineer. In all events, where better in the world to be on a glorious evening in early summer than along this fabulous shoreline with its wooded bays and reedy little nooks, teeming with bird life? There was a silence of total contentment in the boat as we gently drifted along.

I had reeled in my dapping line a few minutes earlier, preferring to just relax and enjoy the warmth of the evening sun and now, through half closed eyes, I noticed a slightly anomalous movement in the water twenty yards downwind and maybe ten yards outside the line of the drift. Interesting. Could be a fish.

We had brought along our dry fly rods that day and the cork handle of my rod was right beside me, so with a self-encouraging grunt of *why not*, I picked it up, worked out some line, and tossed the spent gnat towards the possible rise. 'Thought I saw something down there', I explained, as my two companions watched. Three interested pairs of eyes on the fly, hoping for a reaction. Suddenly, a nice quiet take and the gnat had gone. Surprised, I struck, leaning backward to pick up the little belly of slack that I had lazily allowed to form as the boat drifted along. Solid resistance, and a fine trout, dark and handsome, leapt defiantly out of the water before taking off in a powerful run that put a healthy bend in the nine foot rod. On the light tackle the fish went wild, stripping line off the reel like there was no tomorrow, and when he turned back toward the boat I found myself frantically hand lining slack onto the floorboards as I tried to keep some sort of contact with him.

Five minutes later a lovely trout of just under three pounds slid over the net and ensured that never again would we take to the lake during the mayfly without the dry fly rods.

***

A few evenings later, not having had any success on the gnat in the meantime, Michael and I found ourselves meandering along behind the Corrikeen islands as evening fell over the lake. It had been another lovely day and there were plenty of gnats going out all over the lake so that it was difficult to know exactly where to go to find a feeding fish. What little breeze was there was from the north, and a broad slick about a hundred yards wide extended from the calm water in the lee of the islands down the lake towards Ryan's Point. There was certainly no chance of a dap so most of the other boats had gone ashore. We could just make out one or two in the dark shadows of the trees on the Clare side and one other at the far end of the Corrikeens themselves.

Although there were plenty of gnats and the odd brown sedge on the calm water behind the island, nothing stirred to them. It was just nice to be there and we waited close to the reeds for a half an hour or so, paddling slowly back out for a few yards every so often to check that there was nothing moving further out. But as the light slowly faded we saw nothing. Surely if anything was going to show it would be here, in this quiet place near the reeds.

Eventually, as a first move home towards Dromineer, we decided to follow the slick out for a few hundred yards. Michael stood in the stern, watching and listening, as I paddled slowly backwards in the dwindling light. Here and there in the stillness, a grebe or a duck caught our eye in a fish-like dive, but there was no sign of a trout. Until out of the blue Michael pointed and said, *'There, something over there!'* We quietly eased the boat to a stop, peering down the slack water, and quite suddenly, very close to us, there was a very positive rise. The fish was too close for us to get a fly to him before he was on top of the boat so we stayed put and waited to see would he come again. He rose again, this time upwind of the boat, and we watched him take several more gnats before we lost sight of him in the half-light. Within a few minutes another fish rose in front of us on the slick, maybe forty yards or so away. This time we were ready and as we watched him take a few more flies, moving over and back across the still water but coming closer all the time, we cast out our two gnats and waited.

It suddenly became apparent that there were two or three fish down there in front of us. They were feeding well, often showing their backs and tails as they cruised slowly through the feast of gnats with enormous confidence. We were trembling with anticipation, trying to get a fly close to them, but their pattern was entirely unpredictable as they moved irregularly around the boat, just beyond our casting range. One thing we were certain of - they were very big trout indeed. Many of the rises were typical quiet, dimply gnat rises. But every now and then we saw the full length of a massive trout as it rose slowly and leisurely to take a fly. And a couple of times there was a tremendous surge in the water as something disturbed one of them, perhaps a big pike or a rival getting too close to be tolerated.

It was nail-biting stuff but we just could not get close to them. Any time we tried to ease the boat within casting range of one of them, it simply turned away and continued to feed away from the boat. They seemed to be fully aware of our presence and not too concerned by us as long as they kept their distance. We certainly didn't put them down. Just once a fish took a fly close to one of ours on what seemed like a certain interception course but he just curled quietly under our artificial without touching it and continued to feed away from us again having caused a couple of near heart attacks.

Then with uncanny suddenness they all stopped and it was over. We sat there for ten minutes, impressed by what we had seen. These were *enormous* trout. Double figures, some of them, we were sure. The good news was that they were definitely feeding on gnat because many times we had tracked a particular fish and clearly saw the next gnat on his path go down. On the other hand, apart from that single occasion when one of them curled below our fly, we knew full well that we hadn't got close enough to any of them to cover him properly. They were too smart, too aware that we were there, to let us get close. As we motored back across the lake towards the lights of Dromineer we reminded ourselves of the fish we had caught on the gnat a few days earlier. Where there was one willing fish, there surely would be others.

***

The following day we had our first real planned success with the gnat. Conditions were different to the previous night at the Corrikeen islands. The breeze was now just a little stronger and from the northwest so we headed further up the lake towards Islanmore knowing that there were plenty of options around the big circular island no matter what the vagaries of the wind might be. We stood on the shore at seven o'clock, drinking coffee and planning our strategy for the evening. The day had again been warm and a few gnat had been trickling out all the time, but now they were dancing everywhere along the shore and were starting to go out in numbers. The wind had remained fairly steady in direction and there was a nice well defined narrow slick stretching from a huge boulder on the shore right across towards the point of Islanbrien. In deference to our experiences of last evening, we decided to concentrate on this slick. Unless the slick broke up, we agreed, we would stick to this game plan for the evening.

We pushed quietly out through the reeds onto the start of the slick, picked up our rods and waited. Already there were quite a few gnats on the water. They seemed to collect on the slick rather than in the ruffled water to either side, or maybe it was just easier to see them there, but we saw no sign of a rise. Michael pushed the boat slowly backwards along the calm water while I stood in the stern keeping watch.

About a hundred yards out from the reeds we met the first fish. We heard him first, just a little *slurp* somewhere in front of us, and then saw him quietly take another gnat about twenty yards down the slick. Another rise, five feet to one side, and we realised immediately that there were two fish feeding together and they were coming towards us fairly quickly. They would be on top of us almost before we had time to get our flies out.

Neither our casting nor the boat put them down as they moved past us and continued to take flies, heading back up towards the boulder at the top of the slick. More careful now, we turned the boat broadside on and sat still, waiting to see would there be another fish.

Sure enough, ten minutes later, we again heard a rise before we saw anything and there he was, right hand side of the slick, popping down flies as he fed his way towards us. Out went the two gnats, Michael's down the line towards him, mine towards the centre of the slick in case he changed direction. This was a real chance, and we were ready for him. He took another fly about a foot short of Michael's. I could hear the sharp intake of breath as the adrenalin surged, and down went his gnat in a nice quiet, confident take. Michael struck immediately but never even touched the fish as the fly came straight back to him.

We hadn't time to be disappointed. Another fish was moving up the slick towards us and again we covered him perfectly. Again the gnat was taken but the speedy strike failed to connect. Either we were doing something wrong or the fly was not exactly to their liking. We thought about this. These were very slow, confident rises and it was clear that the fish were doing everything at a very leisurely pace. Perhaps we were striking too fast. We were not giving them a chance to take the fly properly. With that quicker, river-bred strike, we were simply jerking the fly away from the trout before he had a chance to take it down, particularly since he was coming towards us at the time. We would give the next one a little time, treat it almost like a fish taking the dap. Let him down with it.

It worked perfectly. The next fish was well hooked, and the one after, and we ended up with three good fish between us, all in the two and a half pound region. They were all feeding either on the slick or just off the edge of it, and we found that if a fish passed us by without our rising him, we could pull quietly away from the slick and row back to get ahead of him again, just as we did with the dap. We stayed out there until it was no longer possible to see. By then the wind had collapsed altogether and the whole lake was like the proverbial millpond and even then we could still hear the occasional sipping rise not far from the boat.

***

Eventually we called it quits and headed back in the dark towards Dromineer. It had been a wonderful evening's fishing, we had a lot to tell George, and it was dangerously near closing time as we pushed into the busy pub, almost too late for a drink. We finished our first pint in a flash and, as his other law-abiding customers started to leave, the landlord reluctantly agreed to let us have another.

Twenty minutes later, as six happy anglers were discussing the happenings of the day over an equivalent number of freshly pulled pints, the squad car pulled up outside the pub.

'*Its the bloody guards*', moaned the landlord, visions of an endorsement of his licence to sell wines, beers and spirits, and a certain fine into the bargain. But there was nowhere for us to hide and we were caught.

A sergeant, accompanied by a younger guard, strolled into the bar and looked contemptuously at the six of us sitting in front of our pints, pictures of abject guilt. The landlord's attempt to explain the situation was met by a dismissive wave as the sergeant frostily enquired if we knew what time of the night it was, or whether indeed we had any homes to go to.

There were no excuses. We had been "found on", as the saying goes, and it would cost us a day in court, a fine, and the indignity of seeing our names in the local newspaper.

With a curt nod of his head, the sergeant motioned to the younger guard to take our names. Out came the notebook as he walked purposefully over to George, whom he had known as a pal since school days. 'Now then,' said the guard, almost apologetically licking his pencil, and with more than a hint of a smile on his innocent face, 'could I have your name please, George'!

The magic of the moment was definitely worth the fine.

***

One evening a couple of years after our adventures with the big trout at the Corikeens, Michael and I were over on the Clare side of the lake hoping for a good evening's gnat fishing. Gnats had been going out sporadically all day and we had covered quite a few rising fish with no success. It was a bit unusual for us to be so consistently refused and, as usual, this meant a lot of chopping and changing of flies.

Among the assortment of spent gnats in my box there was one strange little creation that was definitely different. I had found it in a tackle shop in a tray of more typical black gnats, but it was a little smaller than the others, with a definite ginger tinge in the hackle. It may have started life on the tying vice as a spent Lake Olive, but it was bigger than an olive ought to be, and its body was of cream quill. For some reason it had caught my eye and I bought it, and that afternoon, after missing yet another fish, its moment finally came and I tied it on.

The result was immediate and spectacular. The first fish I covered took it straight away with a lovely, confident rise. I tightened up and sure enough instead of the fly coming back to me from an inch below the surface, there was a good solid connection from a foot or so down, and he was on.

The next fish did the same thing, and in the meantime Michael's conventional black gnat was still getting the cold-shoulder treatment, either being totally refused or just slightly drowned in a halfhearted rise. The little fly worked a treat and within a few days it had accounted for half a dozen nice trout and was showing terminal signs of wear and tear. The tail whisks had been chewed off and the ginger hackle had started to unravel so I carefully stowed what was left of it in a box for future reference.

I was working in a potash mine in the north east of England at this time, and on the way back home at the end of each mayfly season I invariably called in to John Hanlon in Garnett and Keegan's wonderful fishing tackle shop in Dublin's Parliament Street. I brought the tattered remnants of the ginger gnat to him and asked would he have his experts make me a dozen of them, with appropriate tail of course. He was very interested in the litany of its successes and assured me that the copies were as good as tied.

About a month later a puzzled postman in England brought me a small package with a green customs label bearing the mysterious legend, *Dry Flies - Carefully Tied in Ireland.* Inside were the dozen gnats, perfect replicas of the original (which was also enclosed), with exact ginger tinted hackle and cream body, and of course a perfect three-whisked tail.

For several years we fished that gnat in preference to any other, and with great success too. Although it was much smaller than the natural flies, it was remarkable how fish would pick it out from among any number of real spents on the water. Not only that, but it was likely to rise a fish at any time of the day, even in the morning before any gnat were actually about.

My most unusual experience of this happened one morning when I was staying down on the shore at Youghal Bay. On this beautiful, sunny morning I was ready to set off for Dromineer at 9.45 a.m. I had my dry fly rod set up in the car, just a matter of pushing the two pieces together, and I debated momentarily whether I would take a look at the little quay, which was just a few yards away through the alders, and maybe have a few casts, or whether I would listen to the ten o'clock news on the car radio while driving to Dromineer to meet the others for the day. The sweet smell of hawthorn blossom and grass and the murmuring sound of lapping water from through the trees was too much for me! Just a look, I said to myself, taking the rod and walking quietly down to the pier.

The breeze was blowing obliquely inward from the lake and there was a nice wavelet passing by the end of the tiny pier and in towards the shore. Almost immediately, about twenty yards downwind from where I stood, I saw a nice rise, a fish obviously travelling upwind, obliquely away from the shore towards the end of the pier. I started working out some line and before I got the fly out, up he came again, nearer to me. Out went the ginger gnat and I only had to wait a couple of seconds before there was a good solid rise and I was in him. He was almost three pounds and my pals in Dromineer couldn't believe it when I produced him later. A fish in the boat before lunch was always a great bonus, but to get one before we ever got an oar wet was something really special.

There were many other occasions when we caught good fish casting from the shore with either the ginger gnat or the more conventional black-hackled one. One of the most enjoyable moments of any fishing day was often to be had during the break ashore for grub. We always pulled in to a sheltered shore for our break, and on a sunny day it could be a real pleasure to just relax in the heat and watch the dancing gnats - and keep an eye for movement on the calm water in front of us. Often we would see a trout cruising quietly around in the slack water, mopping up anything that was there. Sedges, struggling partly hatched mayflies, the odd dead gnat; he'd take almost anything that was there. After cleaning his patch out he might disappear for maybe half an hour to allow more goodies to accumulate and then, suddenly, there he would be again, pop-popping his way around his beat in the sultry heat of the day. Sometimes he would be working a circular beat, taking him close to the shore at some point. If you were patient and waited for him to reach the near-shore point of his beat, you had a great chance of rising him.

After a few years of success with the ginger gnat it suddenly went out of favour with the trout and we could see no reason for this. We had had a couple of batches of them tied through John Hanlon and the pattern remained unchanged. We compared the current specimens with some of the original batch that were kept, tailless and bedraggled heroes of the past, in a spare box, and they looked the same, in particular the all-important ginger hackle and the quill body. But for some reason the trout were not impressed any more, the ginger gnat became history, and we reverted to the more traditional black-hackled spents again.

***

There was one special day when we were fishing with Val along the Skehana shore, a few miles up the lake from Dromineer. Val had been back in Ireland for a few years and he really loved Lough Derg, particularly for the fantastic bird life that is so prolific on the islands and along the unspoilt shoreline.

It was a wonderfully warm, sunny day, and after a very leisurely lunch, it was lovely to just stretch out and rest among the gorse and heather. We were all soon half asleep, except for Val who was watching the movements of a tiny greenish-yellow bird that was flitting agitatedly from bush to bush, apparently not at all happy with our presence. It was a willow-warbler, and by her behaviour Val reckoned we must have been almost sitting on her nest.

She came and went a dozen times or more, and eventually appeared with three or four mayflies in her beak. After watching us suspiciously for a few more minutes she flew down almost onto Val's feet, and disappeared under a little tuft of heather.

She left her nest again after a few minutes and Val brought us forward to take a peep at the tiny family. On the ground under the heather, a brilliantly constructed nest of tightly woven grass and moss, partially covered by a perfect dome-shaped roof. Peering carefully we could see five or six tiny beaks trustingly craning towards us for food. It was so brilliantly concealed, and so dangerously accessible to ground predators - including ourselves, as we must have clumped around it gathering firewood. Feeling like intruders, we carefully gathered up our things and tiptoed away, leaving the little nest in peace.

That evening, a gentle breeze from the south east was taking the spent gnats from the bushes on Cameron Island onto a perfect slick that stretched towards the Bunbury, a rocky shallows about three hundred yards off shore. Inside the rocks there is a lagoon about forty yards wide and a couple of feet deep. It was dry fly heaven and two of us were taking turns to fish towards a glorious sunset while the third sat at the oar and simply surrendered to an idyllic summer's evening.

In a sheltered little nook among the Bunbury rocks, two big trout were taking gnats at their spectacular leisure. They were almost motionless, like stationary submarines, with their backs and dorsal fins clear of the shallow water, and every now and then one of them would idle slowly forward to suck in a fly with the lazy deliberation of a giant goldfish in a pond. Michael spent about ten minutes casting very carefully until one of the fish glided forward and just inhaled the fly. The commotion in the quiet little sanctuary was explosive as the trout panicked, looking for a way out through the rocks. Michael managed to keep him under control and eventually landed a block of a trout weighing nearly four pounds.

We fished on for another hour, until well after the sun had dipped behind the shadowy hills of Clare and the light gradually faded to that ethereal, almost tangible texture of a summer's night on water. Until all the gnats had gone, and the only sounds were of moorhens and coots fussing among the reeds, and the occasional lowing of cattle in the distance.

It was to be Val's last visit to Lough Derg before he finally succumbed to a long illness, and it was fitting that it had been such an outstanding day. *'You know'*, he said, standing in the stern of the boat and looking in total contentment at the stillness and the beauty of the lake in the fading light, *'if you were to write away to ask for a day, you'd look for one like this'*.

***

It was on an evening in 1994 that we met the big trout at Hazel Point, the event that is described in the Prologue. After we hooked him, the trout made a couple of long, nerve-jangling runs before settling down into a dogged fight around the boat. For a while I didn't really believe that he was as big as we had imagined when we had first saw him coming towards us up the slick. Maybe this saved me from collapsing with a fit of nerves, although Michael did tell me afterwards that my legs were visibly shaking during the fight.

The most dramatic moment came after about twenty minutes when we got our first real look at the fish. He was close in to the boat but deep down and out of sight, the entire ten feet of leader under the water. I could tell that he wasn't tired and I didn't really want him there so close to the boat with all its potential dangers, but at that stage *he* was very much in charge. The pressure began to ease on my arm and I saw the end of the fly line come out of the water and the leader begin to emerge. He was coming up and Michael and I stood silently and anxiously together and watched. He came up slowly and slightly on his side, and I will never forget the mixture of feelings - fear, apprehension, dread, helplessness - as this huge, golden shape materialised in front of us. Michael is a rock-solid character, with many very good trout to his credit, and when I heard his exclamation, I *knew* that this was no illusion, this was indeed something special.

He must have seen us then because he suddenly took off again, thankfully away from the boat, and for the only time he jumped, only about two rod lengths away from us, and on a dangerously tight line. Before the fish had reached the zenith of his jump, my brain had registered the danger, told my arm to lower the rod, and it was done. He hit the water on a slack line, the splash almost reaching the boat, and off he went with the reel screaming its approval of a danger past. 'Well done' muttered Michael, and the two of us breathed again.

By the time we got him into the boat I was a nervous wreck. We shook hands and clapped each other on the back and admired the trout. Half an hour, Michael told me, pointing to his watch. I had been amazed by the power of the fish and I knew that I would never have landed him without Michael's help. It was definitely down to both of us.

He weighed seven pounds fourteen ounces, and that night in the Whiskey Still there were three trout of over seven pounds laid out on the black Liscannor flagstones, all caught on dry fly. One of them was caught by our friend Pat McGrath on the same slick as ours, half an hour earlier. Cameras flashed and pints of stout passed over and back across the bar as a great celebration went on. The three big trout were a tribute to Lough Derg, a display of what she could produce, and it was great to be a part of it.

The trout now lives in a glass case in our dining room on the far side of the room from an east facing window, forever swimming through a few slanting reeds growing from a timeless sandy bottom. Through most of the year the morning sun is too high in the sky to reach across the room and illuminate the case. But in mid December, as the year approaches the solstice, the sun is low enough and first thing in the morning it shines directly onto the fish, highlighting the beautiful markings as fresh and stark as they were that evening in May. We named him after the five thousand year old passage tomb in County Meath, where the dawning rays of the winter solstice sun creep along the passage below the mound to illuminate the deepest chamber of the tomb spectacularly. He's affectionately known as *Newgrange!*

***

In 1995 we met what could have been our biggest trout ever. Michael and I were down along the Urra shore hoping to atone for a few very poor days with a late evening fish on spent gnat. Conditions were not perfect by any means. It was cold, with a stiffish breeze from the south west almost parallel to the shore, and the water looked rough and dark and thoroughly uninviting. We figured that any gnat going out from the trees further along the shore would not make it far in the cold wind but would be blown down this way. If so, maybe some crazy fish might show an interest. Although there were a few gnats on the water, there were no slicks or calm patches to collect the flies, no focal point where a fish might choose to feed, and by about nine o'clock we hadn't seen sight or sign of a rise. It looked like another blank day, our interest was rapidly declining in the cold, and we were planning that first pint in the welcoming warmth of the pub.

Out of the blue, and much to our surprise, we saw a substantial rise about fifty yards downwind of us and about forty yards to the left. And again, coming fast. A fish was feeding up towards us but he was going to pass much too far to one side for us to cover him. Michael started to push hard with the trailing oar to try to back us left but the fish was travelling so fast that he was past us before we could move far enough sideways to get a fly to him. As he travelled away up the wind he was hammering into the flies more like a fish taking sedges or mayflies rather than sipping down spent gnats. Quickly reeling in, Michael swung out the second oar and started to back the boat upwind after the trout with me in the stern, false casting and watching for a chance to cover the fish. He was still taking gnat with the big, bulging rises of a fish that is moving fast close to the surface but he was travelling at a hell of a pace, as fast as a man could walk, and Michael was having to back-paddle hard with both oars to try to keep up with him.

Although we were keeping pace with the big trout, and he was keeping on an almost straight line, I couldn't get the fly down in front of him properly without "lining" him and risking putting him down. He was going so fast that if I tried to get the fly within the length of the cast of his nose, he was past it before he had a chance to see it. We had followed him for maybe a hundred yards by this time and I was getting desperate. I had put the fly down to him about ten times but each time he rose almost immediately on the far side of it, travelling hard away from us.

Then suddenly the trout turned abruptly left, taking first one fly and then another. Michael saw the change of direction immediately and stopped paddling. Scarcely believing my luck I made the now much easier cast and dropped the fly a couple of feet left of the last take. I wondered would the fish have resumed his old line away from us again. Both of us were glued to the fly - we had watched the fish take maybe thirty gnats as we followed him up the shore and we felt like Ahab with the white whale. There was just a moment's delay and he rolled straight through the fly, head and tail showing as he took it and continued on his way. There was dead silence as I gave him a moment or two to take it properly and then tightened firmly into him. The reaction was instant and, uniquely in my experience, completely and utterly irrepressible. As the rod was almost torn from my hand in two or three violent wrenching pulls, we saw a very large golden-brown body break the surface in a mass of spray and water. And with that, he was gone.

I looked at Michael, wondering did he too realise that this had been a really big fish. I think he felt the loss even more that I. *'That was a close encounter!'* he said, shaking his head in disbelief. Certain I had been broken, I reeled in. The fly was still there, point and barb of the hook both intact.

Neither of us had much doubt that this was a double figure fish, much bigger than anything we had ever caught before. In all likelihood the fly had been taken reasonably well but had simply bounced off the hard mouth of the fish.

There wasn't much talk in the boat as the outboard pushed us homeward along the dark wooded shoreline in the cold and rain. Four blank days in a row, and now this disappointment. I caught Michaels eye as he squinted into the rain from the stern, his hand on the tiller of the outboard. He grinned sympathetically and shrugged, shouting across the noise of the engine, *'Ah well! Isn't it grand to know he's there?'*

We laughed, and had to agree that it was!

The Magic of Lough Mask

The hatches of mayfly on Lough Derg begin earlier than on most of the other Irish lakes. Around the 5th or 6th of May, sometimes even as early as late April, the first welcome flies are seen in Luska Bay and the word goes out to anglers to check out the rods and dust off the fly boxes. On the other limestone lakes to the north the hatches are progressively a few days later so that Lough Corrib, for instance, is maybe ten days later in starting, and Lough Mask a day or two later still. There are odd exceptions to that, like Lough Carra, a near neighbour of Mask, where hatches begin as early as Derg due to the unique nature of the lake's marly bottom and the fact that it is extremely shallow and heats up more quickly in the rising spring temperatures. In any one lake the hatches will continue for about three weeks so that a really dedicated angler can follow the action up along the country for perhaps six weeks in any season.

In 1977 I was late getting home from the potash mine in England for my much anticipated week's fishing and when I got to Dromineer I found that the mayfly was all over for the year. It was early June, very warm weather, and not only had the hatches ended about a week earlier, but just about all the gnat had already gone out as well. In addition, the trout had turned their attention to feeding on perch fry, which in nature's economical scheme of things become freely and abundantly available just as the mayfly finishes. This always marks a temporary end to the trout fishing as it is virtually impossible to imitate these tiny transparent fish with an artificial, and even if you could, your imitation would be lost among the countless millions of the little creatures. The trout feed on them with a vengeance, often two or three big fish working together to herd the shoals around as they gorge themselves. Although it is tremendously exciting to watch, fishing becomes a frustrating dead loss.

In desperation I rang my old fishing friend, Ruaidhrí, who lives near Ballinrobe in County Mayo, and he assured me that he would be delighted if I came for a few days - and that I would not be disappointed with my first visit to Lough Mask. We had fished together through many years and had enjoyed the Corrib and other places together in the past. Ruaidhrí had moved to the west a few years earlier and was totally captivated by Mayo and its people, and I could sense on the phone that he was eager for an opportunity to share this lovely place with me.

I had never seen Mask before and I was not disappointed. The Ballinrobe side of the lake is pure limestone country, and the lake margins are spectacularly wild, with rocky shorelines and ragged limestone reefs of almost wilderness type splendour. The western side of the lake, the Tourmakeady side, is made of sterner, older rocks and the Partry Mountains form a beautiful backdrop to the lake.

Ruaidhrí was not on holidays at the time so I planned to do some shore fishing until he was free to take a boat out on the Saturday. On the first evening we drove down to Aughinish Bay, a few miles north west of Ballinrobe, to enjoy a couple of hour's shore fishing together. It was a fine, summery evening with a nice breeze blowing from behind our casting arm. We were both well used to shore fishing from our evenings on the reservoir with the murragh, so we felt quite at home and this bay looked ideal. Although there was only an odd mayfly to be seen, and no spent gnat, I decided to put up the ginger spent which at that time was still very much in favour on Derg.

We had a great evening's fishing and my impression was that the Mask trout were much more inclined to feed on the surface than their brethren on Derg. Between the two of us we had three fine trout totalling almost eight pounds and we were two happy anglers afterwards, sitting with a pint in Dermot O'Connor's bar in Ballinrobe and chatting about times past. It was great to see Ruaidhrí again and I was hugely impressed with Lough Mask.

***

The following day produced one of those unforgettable experiences that happen all too rarely in a lifetime, often not at all. The weather chart had shown a high pressure area centred off the north west coast which would give a hot, sunny day with a light breeze from the south east and, sure enough, it was a glorious summer's morning and with Ruaidhri gone to work, I was in no hurry to get to the lake.

After a leisurely breakfast I headed off at about one o'clock and parked the car at the bottom of the little bohereen that takes you to Aughinish Bay. From a fishing point of view the day looked like a dead loss. It was already stiflingly hot with the sun blazing down from a cloudless sky and just the gentlest of breezes. It was simply a day to laze about in the sun, to enjoy the birdsong and the smell of the gorse, and do nothing but relax. Unhurriedly I tied on the ginger gnat and mooched along the rocky shore in my waders to a point where a reef of limestone formed a narrow islet about twenty yards out from the shore and parallel to it.

The landscape here was incredible. Thick beds of grey limestone formed a platform of bare rock that had shattered along a fracture system into huge, elongated blocks, parallel to the direction of the bay. One of these blocks formed the reef-like islet that had caught my eye. It looked like a very interesting spot and I stopped there. Quite obviously, the submerged rocky terraces below the water would have the same chaotic character and there would be deep gorges, shallow reefs and weird little nooks and crannies everywhere, ideal haunts for a big pike or a trout. On this magnificent summer's day I had this paradise to myself - there wasn't another sinner in sight.

With the bright sun over my left shoulder I could see lots of detail in the water in front of me. It was not possible to wade out very far as the bottom was a jumble of boulders with deep water in between them. A step off a nice flat boulder could suddenly take you into three or four feet of water, well over your waders. The rocks were weathered and etched into all sorts of grotesque shapes: pits and grooves with razor sharp little ridges and spurs. The best I could do was to find a good flat solid rock, put my net down beside me, and use that as a base to fish from.

As I stood there working out the options I saw a very innocuous-looking rise a few yards off the left edge of the reef outside me. There was an odd mayfly hatching in the shallows, but I couldn't be sure what the fish had taken. Within a couple of minutes he rose again, another insignificant show, and I cast the fly out towards him, helped by the little breeze. The ginger gnat sat nicely on the sparkling water and I let it sit there until the breeze straightened the line and the fly started to drag slightly, before picking up carefully and casting again. My cast was taking the fly about a yard beyond the flat calm and into the slightly riffled water just beyond the shelter of the shore.

No further sign of the fish so I picked up and cast a third time. This time, just as the fly was about to drag again, there was a small splashy rise as you might expect from a little *brickeen* - and the ginger gnat was gone. I was very surprised but automatically I did what we had learned to do with the big fish on Derg. I hesitated momentarily before ripping in the slack line with my left arm and simultaneously lifting the rod firmly with my right in a very deliberate strike, expecting at best a small fish to fly over my shoulder into the gorse bushes. Instead, there was a very solid resistance and something started to move inexorably to my left in quite an unhurried way, away from the reef. I felt straight away that this was a big fish and the drowsy apathy of a moment ago was replaced by absolute focus and concentration. I checked to make sure that my net was easily reachable and began to take stock of my position as the fish continued moving slowly and deliberately to my left before turning abruptly back towards the reef again.

For about twenty minutes the trout just kept on moving up and down outside me over a distance of maybe thirty yards or so, never far from the rocky islet. My big fear was that he would move outside and behind the reef, in which case there could only be one outcome. I couldn't really shift my own position to move further from trouble because of the deep holes between the boulders I had stepped across to get to where I was. If I tried to do that I would have been unable to take the net with me, and there was always the chance that I would have lost my footing in doing so anyway. So I had no choice but to play him from where I stood, perched like a heron on my rock in the sun.

By this time it was definite that I was into a really good fish. Nothing I did seemed to encourage him to change his tactics as he moved first to the right, then back over the same territory to his left. I looked desperately up and down the shore to see was there anybody around who might be able to help me, even a distant boat, but I was on my own.

Eventually he tired a bit and I managed to persuade him to come towards me a little, now well inside the reef. At least from there he was unlikely to get the far side of the jagged rocks and I felt that perhaps there was some chance of landing him. Again I checked the net and it was easily reachable with the handle turned conveniently towards me. Things were going my way.

He never once jumped or showed himself as he swam up and down outside me. My arm was tiring as I kept the strain on him, but he was coming closer all the time. I was getting very edgy now as I became more convinced that this was probably one of the best trout I had ever hooked. The dangerous part was yet to come, when I had to bring him into the shallower water, in among the rocks, but he was nowhere near ready for that yet. He was still playing quite deep down and I hadn't caught any sight of him at all.

Suddenly he changed his tactics. He moved away to my left as before, but this time he was travelling obliquely in towards the shore. I held the rod as high as I could and bent it into him to keep him, and the line and cast, above the hidden rocks and he responded and came back towards me, now only a few yards out from my own rock. As he got level with me I could see the cast running almost straight down into the water but I could see nothing of the fish. About half of the cast was showing so I guessed he was about three or four feet under the surface still. A few yards in front of me I could see two big tabular blocks of limestone that had obviously once been together. The original rock had obviously cracked and separated and the tops of the two components were about two feet under the surface in maybe five or six feet of water. Where the two sides had toppled apart there was a vertical gap about a foot wide, just enough to allow a big fish through. I groaned to myself as the fish turned slightly and headed straight for the dark channel. *Go over them, please,* I prayed as I applied as much upward pressure as I dared to coax him over the needle-sharp rocks. But almost as if he had known what he was doing all along, he went straight into the gap. There was just a slight jerk and then a dead weight and that was that. No commotion in the water, no swirl, no sign of any panic. As the numbing realization of what had happened sank in, I kept a strain on the rod, hoping somehow that the trout was still there, waiting for the sudden kick as he took off out towards the reef again. But he was gone, and my ginger gnat was stuck fast in one of the two rocks.

I felt sick with disappointment. I knew it was a big fish. It was almost half an hour since I had hooked him and I hadn't even tired him enough to get a look at him. It had been so near, if only those two rocks hadn't formed that funnel for him to escape through. If only I'd had the *bottle* to keep him up over the rocks. In hindsight there would have been nothing to lose, it was six of one and half a dozen of the other. But I didn't, and the nylon cast must have caught on the rock and the big trout's momentum just pulled the fly away from him.

I tugged a few times on the snagged fly but it was stuck fast, so I walked back across the few rocks to the shore, paying line out as I went and swearing softly to myself. One thing I was sure of, I may have lost the fish but I wasn't going to leave my gnat out there as well. No bloody way!

I looked up and down the deserted shore, pulled off waders, socks and trousers, picked up the rod and started to walk gingerly out across the rocks to recover the fly. I could feel the sharpness on my bare feet, but I kept going, stubbornly determined to get the gnat back. The holes between the rocks were quite deep and I got wet to my waist, but I made it to the two rocks that had saved the trout, reached down the line for over an arm's length, and freed the fly which was stuck in the corally layer of the rocks surface. As I winced my way carefully back towards the shore I knew that I had cut my feet, but it wasn't until I was in shallow water that I realised just how much. They were bleeding quite badly and I could feel the pain as I surveyed the damage. *If I had worn the bloody waders*, I told myself angrily, *I would have saved my feet, and the boots would have dried again in half an hour anyway!*

When I got myself dried out I decided to fish on anyway, until by six o'clock my feet were so sore that I just had to stop.

I had a good rueful look behind me as I got into the car and headed back to tell Ruaidhrí of my escapade.

***

My feet had been cut quite badly on the sharp limestone rocks and when I had put my socks on again, the dye had caused an infection in the cuts. The next day I was in a lot of pain so I went to a doctor - an angler himself - who, on hearing the story, suggested that I might have behaved a little more intelligently. He ordered antibiotics and no standing on the feet, so Ruaidhrí and I were glad to take a boat out that day, Saturday, and although we had a couple of fish, there was nothing of the excitement of the previous two days on the shore.

We were back in O'Connor's bar that night for a couple of farewell pints, and as usual there were lots of anglers there. I told my story of the lost trout to two of Ruaidhrí's friends, not expecting any great sympathy, but they listened with great interest to what I said. They asked me to describe in detail the place in Aughinish Bay where it had happened. I could do this precisely. I knew how far along the shore I had gone from where the bohereen ended, and the reefy islet was a perfect landmark. I'd never forget the place. They nodded understandingly, almost as if they knew before I told them. They also knew the precise place! And they told me that my trout was a well known resident of that spot, had been hooked and lost several times by boat anglers, but had always used the reef to effect his escape, had broken them every time. The consensus among all was that he was at least eight pounds weight, maybe more. It had indeed been a near miss for me!

***

182

About ten years after the Aughinish Experience I got the chance of another few days on Mask and, needless to say, I grabbed it with both hands. It was early June again, and the mayfly was in full swing as four of us headed off from County Meath to spend the Whit weekend in Sean's holiday home on the shore of the lake. Since Sean was a teetotaller, we all travelled together in his car. The trip to the pub in the evening would be several miles, and the rest of us enjoyed a pint or two after the day's fishing. Although he didn't drink at all himself, he enjoyed the *craic* in the pub as much as any of us and he would be delighted to run us in each evening.

I fished with Sean and we saw very little action on the first day. By about five o'clock we had nothing in the boat and we had hardly seen a rise all day. This wasn't in the script for Lough Mask. As we drifted through a gap between two small islands a nice looking fish rose about forty yards ahead of us. Red alert; this would break our duck. He rose again, this time only about twenty yards in front of us, dead on the line of our drift, and we were sure we were in business. The boat drifted on, both of us concentrating fiercely, and just as our flies were over his expected position, he rose again about twenty yards further away and obviously now travelling sedately in the opposite direction. This was too much for Sean. 'Come back here you hoor and I'll put manners on you!' he yelled after the trout in injured tones, as the pair of us dissolved into uncontrollable laughter at the prospect.

Now Sean is a brilliant character and I have never known any teetotaller to enjoy a night out in the pub as much as he does. He's lucky. He is naturally good humoured and doesn't require a few pints to raise his spirits at all. Which made it all the more surprising for the other three of us when he announced as we set off in the boats for the second day that he had no intention of rushing ashore this particular evening to drive us to the pub. In those days the pubs in Ireland used to close at ten o'clock on a Sunday night and Sean reasoned that we would have to stop fishing at about eight o'clock to make that deadline. We looked at him, searching for the tell tale signs of a chuckle, but he was serious. We would have to miss our pint, and the fishing chat, and that was very definitely that.

It was a better day, and we all had a fish or two. Coincidentally, President Reagan of the United States was on an official visit to Ireland at the time and he and Nancy were staying that night at Ashford Castle, a very beautiful hotel outside Cong on the northern shore of Lough Corrib, just a few miles away from where we were staying ourselves. The movement of helicopters to and fro around the lake provided extra interest for us during most of the day and we all enjoyed ourselves immensely, but sure enough, Sean stayed out on the lake until about nine o'clock and that, we believed, was the end of the pub.

When we got back to the house Sean pulled out the pan and began to fry rashers and sausages and anything else he could find and presented us with a fabulous meal. By the time we were finished it must have been about eleven o'clock. Suddenly Sean stood up clapped his hands and said, *'Right lads, I'll take ye all for a little drive'*. The three of us looked at him, wondering had he taken leave of his senses. He gave us a wink and a grin, *'Are ye coming?'*

We climbed reluctantly into the car and headed up the tiny bohereen towards the tarred road and Sean swung the car right, towards Cong. When we got to the village it was midnight but to our amazement there were lights on in all the pubs and we could hear the sound of music and song from everywhere. The whole village was celebrating the arrival of President Reagan and Nancy! Sean's face was a picture of delight as he grinned at the three of us toasting him with our first pint. He had known all along that the pubs had been granted an extension for that special evening and he had played us along like the three innocent 'eejits' that we were! We had a marvellous night, proving yet again that the spontaneous night of least expectation is always light years more enjoyable than the one that is carefully planned.

And Sean, with his glasses of Britvic orange, enjoyed it more than anyone!

***

I've been back to Mask a few times since then, and enjoyed good fishing on the lake itself and also down at the fascinating canal than joins Mask to Lough Corrib. The canal was excavated in an attempt to form a navigable link between these two great lakes of the west. A novel idea, but the engineers were never allowed to finish the job. Before the necessary membrane could be laid to prevent the water from disappearing into the mass of fissures and fractures in the limestone, the steam locomotive was invented. All the funds earmarked for canals were diverted towards the creation of a rail network throughout Ireland. The age of steam had arrived. In the case of the Mask to Corrib canal this was good news for the fisherman. What remains is a wonderful place, wild and chaotic, where the river disappears into the wilderness of rock at several locations to create a totally unique effect. Here, you can really feel the freedom and space that is the essence of the west of Ireland. Fantastic exposures of pale grey limestone characterise the area, studded with beautifully fossilised corals; and the canal itself has all the attributes of a truly natural river, and unique ones of it's own. There are very big trout in there, fish that the lake itself would be more than proud of. A few hours spent casting a fly in this almost lost world can produce some surprising results.

A Downward Trend

I don't fish now as much as I used to, and the lessening of my interest has roughly paralleled a gradual decline in the quality of many of our fisheries. Sadly it's true that all over the country, rivers, lakes, ponds and streams have suffered from some degree of pollution and a reduction in fish stocks. Angling, for whatever reason, has lost much of its appeal as a leisure activity. Not so many years ago if you crossed a bridge over any decent river in the country during the fishing season there would be a car or two parked there, and maybe a few bikes as well. Young and young at heart, enjoying their birthright. The riverbanks are quieter now.

I do fish the mayfly still. I wouldn't miss it. For me it goes back so many years to my childhood and the Corrib. To the magic of a special weekend when as kids we would be spirited away from our school books to the rocky shores around Birchall near Oughterard, to fish for fierce, wild trout the likes of which you would never see in the little babbling streams of upland Wicklow.

I lost touch with the Corrib but my great fortune brought me to live for a while close to another mayfly lake, different in character but with great charms of it's own, and wonderful fishing to boot! That was nearly thirty years ago, and though we moved some time ago to live in County Meath, Lough Derg on the Shannon is still an indispensable part of my life.

***

What's the mayfly all about? Fishing, of course, is the essential element that brings the same hopeful anglers back, year after year to try, try again. But there's much more to it than just that.

People make the mayfly what it is. Not just the anglers, but also those who don't fish at all but simply love to be involved in the chat and the *craic* in the pub when the boats are all safely tied up for the night. Or to come out on the lake for a day's fresh air and a barbecued steak like you'd never get in a five star restaurant.

There's also the weather and the time of year. The mayfly gets its name not because it hatches in the month of May, but because the hatches coincide with the flowering of the hawthorn, the magic fairy tree of Irish folklore that we call the May bush. This can happen in May or June, or even in late April, depending on the whereabouts in the country. The mayfly is really a June fly on the Corrib. But whether May or June, it's a wonderful time of year when nature is at its brand new, totally refurbished best. There is such promise in the air of good times to come. I always feel that I head for Lough Derg in the springtime, full of anticipation; but by the time the week is over and I am driving home again, it's suddenly summer and the countryside is filled with the buzzing of hay and silage making machines, and fields of grass stubble gleam golden in the sunshine. Cicely Mary Barker captured this element of transition with lovely simplicity in her lyrical verse about the may blossom:

> "O magic sight, the hedge is white,
> My scent is very sweet;
> And lo, where I am come indeed,
> The Spring and Summer meet."

There's also the freedom from the shackles of time, the absence of newspapers, the big fried breakfasts of rashers and eggs, sausages and puddings that keep you going until four o'clock in the afternoon.

Mind you, the sight of a swirling rise in the sun-glinting wavelets on a beautiful clear morning is not to be sneezed at either. Or the phenomenal hatches of mayfly that defy the imagination for sheer numbers. And in the evening, great hordes of gnats dancing together on gossamer wings along the shore. Until, at some signal known only to them, off they go to fill the air over the lake and ensure that in two year's time the hatches will happen again.

And finally, at the end of a long fulfilling day, to stand at the fireside in the pub and watch the lovingly pulled pints of black stout slowly settle in the glasses on the counter, while the warmth and feeling flood back into fingers and feet. And the stories of the day from up and down the lake begin to unfold around the old wooden counter of the bar.

As we say in Ireland, *Sure where would you be going?*

***

Lough Derg is never an easy lake to fish. You have to work at it, be prepared for many blank days. Fifteen years ago the average catch for our boat of two or three anglers was close to two fish per day. For the boat! Some days could be much better, maybe five or six trout, with an average weight of two or more pounds for each fish. So obviously there were days that were completely blank. Sometimes two, maybe three blank days in a row. You might rise one fish in two days - and you'd better not be dozing at the time. It can happen in the blink of an eye and you don't want to be woken from some comfortable daydream by an urgent, *'Peter, your fly is gone!'* And you tighten up, too late, and your dap is gone and there's nothing there.

We were always very happy with two or three fish in the boat in any single day, with maybe a three or four pounder to really sweeten things up. This was Lough Derg, not Corrib or Mask, and the blank days were part of the deal, somehow enhancing the satisfaction of the days when we did have a few fish. Catching fish every day would become routine. As Michael often philosophically remarked at the end of a fishless day, '*Ah well! It's the bad days that make the good days good*'.

***

By the early nineties, however, our catches had fallen considerably and the average for the boat had dropped to less than one fish per day. Although strangely enough, despite the scarcity of numbers, a larger than usual percentage of trout caught on the lake at that time were very good fish, six and seven pounders. But it was obvious that something was very wrong. All around the lake the same deterioration was observed. In Puckane for instance, a few miles north along the lake from Dromineer, 280 trout were weighed in by the local club during the 1990 mayfly season, and only 40 in 1995. In 1990 the automatic fish counter on the Nenagh River, one of Derg's most important spawning tributaries, registered the passage from the lake of 2,400 trout. In 1997 only 146 trout passed through. The fish were simply not there.

Crucially the quality of the lake water was also deteriorating. Not too long ago we used to make our tea with the lake water. The only concession we made was to fill the kettle well away from the shore to minimise the harmless plankton content. We didn't want soup, we wanted tea. But gradually it became apparent that the quality was suffering and eventually, bowing to the inevitable, a plastic container full of tap water was always taken along for the brew-up.

The major pollutants were known to be agricultural fertilizers, and inadequately treated sewage. Both produce a dramatic enrichment in phosphate and this results in a huge increase in the growth of algae, particularly blue-green algae. The process is known as eutrophication and the result is a deoxygenation of the water by the thriving algae, with consequent disastrous effects on all other living organisms, particularly fish.

At first the effects of pollution were not especially dramatic. Nothing seemed too wrong during mayfly time, but this was before the full heat of summer aggravated the problem each year. The most common visible effects were a slight increase in weed and a reduction in water clarity. Anglers, and others, expressed their alarm, but few listened. Some even predicted that eventually, if action were not taken, there would be fish kills. Surely not on the Shannon with its massive volume of water. But every year the situation got a little worse and no real action was taken by the powers that be to stop the decline. We were, indeed, watching the slow demise of one of Ireland's great fisheries.

In March 1996 thousands of bream were found dead and dying all around the lake. By the time the mayfly hatches began, every shoreline contained the sad remains of dead bream, including many great fish of eight to ten pounds weight. A shocking and depressing waste. Whatever killed them seemed to be quite specific, because no other fish species was affected. Among all the pathetic corpses that we saw during our weeks fishing there was only one small pike, which could have succumbed to one of many other natural causes.

That year towards the end of the mayfly, a couple of days before the Whit bank holiday, Tipperary North Riding County Council erected temporary *Water Unsafe for Bathing* notices along the sandy shores where families traditionally come to paddle and swim. As always, a huge amount of work had been done to prepare these beautiful places for the first really busy weekend of the year, when throngs of happy people would normally come along to enjoy the holiday at the lake. It was sad and disquieting to see. Sailing and boating events were cancelled, business lost, and many people were asking the big question. *Why?*

In 1997 there was a noticeable improvement in the water quality. Water clarity was much better and there was less brown weed on the surface during the warmer days of May. Hopes were high that the corner had been turned and that things were at last under control. As it transpired, there was a worrying reason for this improvement also. At the Ardnacrusha power station near Limerick, engineers checking submerged pipes found that great numbers of a non-indigenous shellfish were encrusting and blocking the pipes. The shellfish was identified as the Zebra mussel (Dreissena polymorpha), a small species native to the Black and Caspian Sea areas, which must have found its way into the lake attached to the bottom of a boat. These small creatures breed at a prolific rate and they have now spread all over the lake and indeed have been identified throughout the entire Shannon system. Each tiny shellfish, about half an inch long, can filter a litre of water through its system each day, and this has a cleansing effect on the water. However, apart from the engineering problems they pose to water pipes, submerged structures and other industrial equipment, they are affecting the ecology of the lake, upsetting the natural balance and interfering with the habitat of bottom dwelling organisms such as nymphs and caddis larvae, and also other shellfish, the basic diet of the big Shannon trout.

***

Fortunately the closure of the swimming areas in 1996 was a very temporary measure and all of the usual water sports were quickly being enjoyed again. There are encouraging reasons to believe that a turnaround has been achieved and a huge public awareness of what is to be lost - or saved - is now evident everywhere. Substantial funds have been allocated to improve ageing sewage treatment plants all over the country, and work has already begun on many of these projects. Industrial enterprises have been made aware that it is no longer tolerable to pollute our waterways in exchange for jobs - a clean environment and good employment can happily co-exist. And, most importantly, the Irish Farmers Association is four square behind a policy of reducing the application of fertilizers on land already over-enriched in minerals. These three efforts, particularly a sensible attitude to fertilizer application, will make a huge difference, but angling and boating clubs, together with local committees and concerned individuals who have done so much vital work in the past, must continue to work hard to ensure that the job is completed. Restoration of Lough Derg and several other important trout fisheries will take many years of effort and investment before the glory days are possible again.

***

When my own four children, Stephanie, David, Nicola and Elva, were small, we had many a great fishing trip together. We would take a picnic to the little river near our home in County Meath and fish for the dashing, handsome brook trout, or just sit in the sunshine and admire the green and blue dragonflies hovering around the yellow irises on a summer's day. It was always a fun thing: never anything too complicated, or so intense that it might stifle any latent fishing interest that could have been there in any one of them. In the summer we used to take a fortnight's holiday in a house on the cliff top overlooking Baltimore harbour in west Cork. From a secluded balcony at the back of the house we had a stunning view away across the harbour and out to Sherkin Island and every time I hear the evocative tinkling of a yacht's rigging against her aluminium mast I am reminded again of those great family holidays we enjoyed so much. We loved to mooch off together to a spectacularly wild place called Beacon Point, to catch mackerel off the rocks and marvel at the big grey Atlantic seals in the heaving swell, watching us watching them!

One afternoon the kids came tumbling up the steps from the harbour, breathless with excitement, to tell Gillian and me that they had seen a conger down at the steps behind the pier. We all rushed down to the harbour steps together, hoping to catch a glimpse of him. Their excitement was totally infectious and I could *feel* their little spirits willing that conger to show himself again, not to let them down. *Please come back; let dad see you!* Suddenly, four sets of pointing fingers, *'There he is, there he is!'* Reflected in their excitement I could see again myself and my brother Dick, two small boys in short pants and sloppy joe tee shirts; at the harbour in Dunmore East all those years before, mesmerized, hardly daring to breath, as a massive conger turned from the step we had just been standing up to our knees in water on, and silently returned to the secret depths of the harbour. Now, a generation later, this other conger passed a few feet below us, wraith-like, blue-grey, gliding effortlessly by with that fascinating undulation. He *was* a big one too, and we watched in collective awe until he gradually faded and finally disappeared into the plankton-haze. It was a very special moment for all of us to share, and amid the wild excitement I realised in astonishment that none of them had ever seen a conger before. Yet they had known exactly what it was from the stories they had heard and the books they had read. I must have done something right! I felt quietly chuffed and very proud, and the magic of the moment will always stay with me.

***

A few years later, Gillian and I decided to introduce a system to encourage the children to earn their pocket money. Good training, we thought! The idea was greeted with a predictable chorus of total disapproval. We allocated a certain remuneration for each of the jobs which we felt were appropriate for the little dears to do, and fiddled the books as necessary to bring the total earnings up to their normal weekly sum. Sometimes, during a week of poor performance, this was fairly difficult, but in all events we recorded each job, and its reward, in a little notebook for them all to see.

Elva, the 'baby', was about seven at the time and in my opinion needed a little more help to achieve her targets than the more senior members of the workforce. On one particular week the entries in the book under her name were conspicuously few, and as Saturday approached there was no way she was going to make the usual grade. Some salvage action was required, so in a moment of inspiration she and I went off to the little river that runs through our town and spent a happy couple of hours fishing for minnows together. When the family inspected the pocket money book on the Saturday to calculate their earnings for the week, there under Elva's name, mixed in with a scattering of washing of dishes and tidying of rooms, was an entry that almost started another World War,

Minnowing, ... *10p*

The resulting furore saw the scrapping forever of the 'Pocket Money Book' scheme, and to this day, in moments of perceived imbalance in the handling of family affairs, I am still contemptuously reminded of the occasion.

***

Although we loved our excursions and adventures to river, lake and sea, none of my children carried any significant interest in fishing through to adulthood. The other requirement obviously wasn't there: the chemistry, the gene that draws you inexorably to the water, compels you to know just what is down there, and how it might be caught.

Hidden at the moment, the gene will surely surface again, some time, in another generation. Another child, another pond, another jam jar full of dreams.

Epilogue

In early May of 1998 I had a phone call from Michael to say that the mayfly fishing on Lough Derg was shaping up to be very poor that year. There had been some good hatches of the green drakes since the end of April, but except for some small fish that were almost certainly "stockies", there was no trout feeding on them. Most of the Derg anglers were heading off for either Corrib or Mask for their fishing. Recently out of hospital after an operation, I decided to give the mayfly a miss and wait for next year's hoped-for revival.

I fished some of my own local rivers in Meath during the late summer. It had been a particularly wet summer so there was lots of water in the rivers and they were clear and clean, where in a normal dry season they would be low and choked with weed. I had some great evenings creeping up along under the high banks and casting a dry fly to these shyest of trout. Even fish that were feeding well would stop instantly if you made the slightest mistake in covering them. The fly had to be dropped right on his nose, even an inch or two short, to coax him to turn and take it. Any sign of line or leader and the game was well and truly up. But cover them correctly and the excitement was intense. Fish of well over the pound in a river less than a rod length wide, careering through the streamers of weed like an express train. It was great fun, but I did miss my days on the lake.

In early September Michael rang again, this time to suggest a couple of days on the Corrib. September is always one of the best fishing months on the big lakes, with the trout feeding well again after the torpor of the summer months. I hadn't fished the Corrib since my days with John Joyce; thirty five years ago I now calculated in astonishment. I really looked forward to seeing it again, but wondered just how much it might have been changed by the passage of so much time.

***

It was a nice fine morning as we started our first drift along the west shore of Inishanbo, the island of the cow. Too pleasant to be a good fishing day, with just a light breeze from the southwest. On the big lakes anglers prefer a good wild day where you will wear your pull-ups non stop or get wet as you motor through the waves between drifts. But this was a morning to enjoy and to savour the splendour of the Corrib again. Away to the west and northwest the mountains of Connemara were as beautiful as anything you could imagine. Close to us were the Maumturks where the western shore of the Corrib nudges into the foothills in little inlets and bays. Behind them in a cluster of incredible concentration, the Twelve Bens looked like something that might have been created as a background to the Garden of Eden.

At lunchtime we were drawn towards the sheltered shore of a nearby island by a tiny plume of smoke. In there we met two young men who had been fishing wet flies for the past ten days and had enjoyed some tremendous fishing. The day before they had caught fourteen trout and kept just five of them, all around the three pound mark. The previous week's catch included a specimen nine pounder. They had just finished their final year at school and were about to take time out to travel the world for a year, working on and off to pay their way. You could sense immediately how they loved and respected the Corrib and how in hands such as theirs it would be safe. It would survive.

We had brought flasks of boiling water and tea bags with us. I looked at the blackened kettle sitting by the embers of their fire and asked the obvious question. Yes, the tea was brewed from the water of the Corrib. Would I like a cup? It was dark and strong and tasted deliciously of wood smoke. I thought how long it had been since we had dared to make tea from the water of Lough Derg that had suffered such abuse through the whole length of the River Shannon. Some day we would do it again.

***

Two glorious fishing days later we said goodbye and Michael headed off for Tipperary. I decided that instead of going directly home myself I would make a detour and take a look again at Aughinish Bay on Lough Mask. I drove up to Maam Cross and turned right down the road towards Cornamona and on through *Joyce Country* into Cong and Ballinrobe. I couldn't count the number of times I had to stop and take out my camera, each time thinking that the new vista was even more stunning than the last one.

Out the Castlebar road from Ballinrobe I found the little road that I had travelled down with Ruaidhrí all those twenty-one years before. Surely this would have changed; I was just lucky on the Corrib.

I stopped the car at the bottom of the bohereen and got out. There was nobody about, just three or four boats pulled up on a gravelly slipway that hadn't been there before, but otherwise it was just the same. The sun was shining brightly, just as it had been when I lost the big trout in the rocks. I took my camera and picked my way up along the shore towards *the spot*. There it was, exactly as I had left it. I tried to remember how I had really felt that afternoon, alone in this spectacular place. I studied the limestone blocks. The upper surface of each and every one was etched by rain and lake water into a mass of solution cavities several inches deep, the rims of which were needle sharp and could be clearly felt even through the boots I had on. Did I really take my waders off and walk barefoot across those to rescue my gnat? I must have been mad.

The wind was from a different point, from the southwest now, so I scrambled on to the other side of the bare limestone reef, sheltered from the light wind. Fifty yards away was a parallel reef, a bare spit of grey limestone pushing out into the lake for two hundred yards with a few stunted bushes growing from the crevices and fissures in the rock. Beyond it, another one, and another as far as the eye could see. In between, narrow clefts of crystal clear water which looked so perfect for fish that I wondered just what you would find if you could magically siphon the water out of one and reveal all. Twenty-pound trout: fifty-pound pike. It could be anything.

Blissfully content in the heat of the sun, I leant against a huge boulder and lit a Hamlet cigar. To my left, across the shining lake, the Partry Mountains slumbered in the summer haze. A few whitewashed cottages nestled in the foothills, thin plumes of blue turf smoke curling lazily into the air. A single white swan worked her way serenely around the point of the reef. Six or seven swallows swooped and dipped in front of me, almost as though they were surprised to see any human being in this wilderness of theirs. I could see small brown sedges dancing in the air along the shore and a few were visible on the calm water before the wind riffle caught it about fifteen yards out towards the next reef. After twenty one years this place still had a unique ambience, an almost primeval atmosphere, that had fascinated me before.

There were quite a few sedges in the air around me now, and more getting caught in the surface film of the calm water all the time. I watched the water more carefully; sensing that here was a situation an opportunistic trout might avail of, all the time becoming more worth his while as more sedges were added. A movement caught my eye, slightly to my left, out towards the edge of the riffle. There he was, right on cue. A good looking trout coming directly towards me across the narrow inlet, taking every sedge in his path in confident popping rises. It was almost as though he wanted to prove something to me: that here, in this special place, everything *was* just as it had been.

Without moving, I watched him come directly towards me until he was only feet away, until he turned and followed the shore towards the point of the reef and the swan. Grabbing my camera off the rock, I started back down the shore, hopping as fast as I could across the tumbled blocks of limestone towards the car and the rod. It would take me maybe twenty minutes to get there, tackle up, and make my way back again through the rocky wilderness. The image of the feeding trout, so clear in my mind, lent wings to my feet. My heart was literally soaring with expectations, like a child again.

The revival of my spirit was complete.

*